THE APPEARANCE OF POWER:
HOW MASCULINITY IS EXPRESSED THROUGH AESTHETICS

TANNER GUZY

TANNER GUZY

Copyright © 2017 Tanner Guzy

All rights reserved. This book or any portion thereof may not be reproduced or reused in any manner whatsoever without the expression written permission of the author except for the use of brief quotations for a book review.

Please send all inquires to: contact@masculine-style.com

First printing, 2017

ISBN-10: 1979138400
ISBN-13: 978-1979138406

www.masculine-style.com

DEDICATION

For my Guzy's. Every day we remind ourselves that we do hard things, good things, kind things, and fun things. Writing this book has been all of those for me. Let it be another reminder to you. This is who we are.

CONTENTS

1	Appearance & Power	1
2	Why Appearance Matters	7
3	Power vs Appeal	25
4	Masculinity & Aesthetics	34
5	Clothing is Communication	53
6	Tactics vs Strategies	57
7	Body	63
8	Archetype	80
9	Tribe	92
10	Taste	110
11	Location	120
12	Effort	129
13	Conclusion	139

1 APPEARANCE & POWER

I have an uncle who lives all alone in a small town in Eastern Idaho. And by small, I mean a population of fewer than 300 people.

He's a reclusive man who would much rather spend time with his dogs and his birds (he's a falconer) than people. In fact, up until this year, the two of us had probably spent fewer than ten total minutes in conversation together.

When it became apparent that my grandmother wasn't going to be with us much longer, my uncle realized he needed to prepare and purchase a suit for her funeral. Knowing that I worked in the industry and having gotten frustrated with the solutions he could find on his own, he reached out to see what I could do for him.

He'd spent a few weeks in various stores but all the suits he was presented with were "too shiny." They didn't look like something he'd wear, made him feel inauthentic, and were making a difficult time even more frustrating for him.

I had my suspicions and, after diving a little deeper with him, I determined a charcoal flannel suit was the best solution. It was serious enough for a funeral, but the traditional outdoor use of flannel also made it rugged enough to be consistent with my uncle and his lifestyle. It was a small win and by no means negated the loss of his mother, but it did help free him up to focus on her, rather than feeling self-conscious about how he looked during her funeral services.

As a thank-you gift for helping him out, he brought me a recently published photo book of the city of Rexburg, Idaho - the town in which he, my mom, and their siblings grew up. In it were a few photos of my various extended family and other shots of different historical sites and important figures in the town's history.

I started to thumb through the book and was quickly drawn in by the clothing of the men. Some photos were from the 19th century, others were during World War II, and there were even some from the early 21st century.

As I was looking at one particular page of war veterans returning home in their uniforms in the 1940's I made the comment of how much I loved the discipline, honor, and diligence that these men exemplified and was demonstrated through their uniforms. The clothes were neatly pressed, fit well, and made them look like dignified war heroes.

My uncle chuckled wryly and said, "Those uniforms hid their lack of those virtues as often as they projected them."

It was a sobering thought. I didn't know the men on these pages. I just saw what they wanted me to see - dignity, discipline, courage, strength - whereas my uncle had spent time growing up around them. He saw things like anger, drunkenness, vice, and weakness.

Power has an appearance and appearance has power. Ideally those two would line up together and the world would be full of good, masculine men who dress and look like good masculine men.

But all too often reality is something different. There are good men and strong leaders out there who dress and look like children or bums. There are awful, lazy men who dress in a way that hides their vices from those around them and makes them appear better than they truly are.

In an attempt to correct these disparities, our current culture tries to rob both appearance of its power and power of its appearance - to say that the way a person dresses or looks doesn't - or at least shouldn't matter.

We're given platitudes like, "don't judge a book by its cover" and there's a often a cultural rush to prove ourselves as non-judgmental as we can.

But, a man's appearance has been an integral part of humanity since before the dawn of civilization. As human beings we use mental shortcuts when assessing our surroundings and the people within them. It is inefficient and dangerous to treat every object, scenario, and person as a blank slate or an unknown.

And, because it is our tendency to judge according to visual stimuli, we use physicality, body language, grooming, and clothing to quickly and effectively communicate who we are and how we want to be perceived.

Some men dress to appear more physically threatening, others to convey status and power within social spheres, some attempt to fit in and not draw attention to themselves, and others use their clothing to show their disdain for the social norms around them.

Regardless of what your intentions are, your clothing says something about you. And no, this doesn't just apply to you, but to every man who has ever interacted with another human being. From the ancient shaman, to the Wall Street banker, the Pope to the gutter punk, all men use clothing and appearance to tell the world who we are. Which means it's worthwhile for you to understand how to use this tool effectively.

This book is not for the guy who's simply looking for an outfit that will help him get laid, nor is it for the man who wants to know the one perfect thing he can wear to nail his job interview.

While it does contain accurate advice, there are no lists of particular items you need to have in your closet, tutorials on how to tie a tie, or breakdowns of why one pair of boots costs $50 and another can be $5000.

Instead, the purpose of this book is to outline the underlying principles of how clothing affects men and masculinity. Understanding and applying those principles will take you far beyond looking like you've been dressed by an image consultant, in one of his five variations of acceptable clothing, and into the realm of being well-dressed all the time.

The ultimate goal of your appearance is to use aesthetics as one of may means to help accomplish your desired ends. Are you trying to find and marry the perfect woman? Clothing won't do it for you, but it can help. On the other hand, if used poorly, your clothing can hinder that pursuit. What about establishing yourself within your career, getting in better shape, making better friends, or any other improvement most of us are interested in? Clothing doesn't do all the heavy lifting, that's still up to you. But it can supplement or counter your other efforts to make yourself a better man.

The key to dressing well is establishing a wardrobe that is consistent with both your realities and your aspirations.

Perhaps you're the kind of man who is content to dress solely in a way that reflects who you are. Do people expect more of you? Do they treat you any better this year than the year prior? Do they help you as you aspire and work to be better or try to convince you that any change you make to your life will either be temporary or not worth it? When people don't see physical evidence of our aspirations, it's easy for them to treat us like they always have and to believe we don't expect anything better of ourselves.

Or, maybe you merely dress to impress but feel as though, if others knew the truth, they'd see you as a fraud - someone without integrity, honesty, or consistency - at least between the appearance you present to the world and the man you truly are. When people don't see any congruence between the person we advertise ourselves to be and really are, they believe us to be dishonest, disingenuous, and untrustworthy.

Dressing well contains an element of both congruence and aspiration. It tells the world, particularly the people who matter most in your world, who you are and where you're headed. It projects honesty and ambition.

This rationale is not to be confused with the idea that your appearance is a primary factor in building status, attracting women, leading other men, taming nature, creating empires, or accomplishing any other masculine goal. While appearance is important, its role is secondary, and any man with a too glaring inconsistency between his appearance and his core characteristics will easily be spotted as a fake.

At the same time, you should treat your style as an aspirational endeavor. We'll dive more into the logistics of this throughout the book but, for now, suffice it to say that whenever you find yourself seeking to improve your station or change your character, one of the easiest and most effective changes is altering your wardrobe.

By making such a visibly drastic change at the beginning of your metamorphosis you will be able to fulfill two different purposes: 1. Communicating your growth easily and directly with those who already know you and 2. Reminding yourself that you are on a mission to be different than the man you once were.

Absorbing the principles within this book will help you understand the historical significance and current importance of the male appearance - how it can be used in dealing both with other men and with women, how it can be used to initiate and complement other aspects of self improvement, how a positive relationship with appearance can improve your life overall, and how to quickly and effectively make the right changes in both mindset and attitude necessary to dressing well.

Do you already have areas in your life where you're powerful? Great! Let's figure out how to build upon or shore up that existing power by improving your appearance.

Are there parts of your life where you wish you had more? Excellent! Then let's start using your appearance - your clothing and grooming - to help you build that up as well as you can.

Your clothing and style won't ever create value for you. The best they can do is magnify it. However, that magnification can be very real and have a dramatic impact on your life.

2 WHY APPEARANCE MATTERS

Men in the Western world have an entirely confused relationship with the way we look.

We either write it off as almost entirely unnecessary and superfluous, give it no attention whatsoever, or we see it as our key defining character trait - all of which place it entirely out of context.

For some reason, we have this false binary in our heads. We see appearance from a moral context as in good vs bad. But the reality is that it exists entirely in the realm of effective or ineffective.

Take, for example, the biggest boogeyman in sartorial circles across the world - cargo shorts.

For the most part, those who prioritize comfort over aesthetics, those who have a lot of gear they need to carry, those who don't put any thought into their appearance and grab the most easily accessible pair of shorts at their nearest big-box store, and those who surround themselves with men who wear cargo shorts, all see this choice as a good one. It's simple, functional, and effective.

On the other hand, those who value aesthetics and tradition, those who don't need the additional pocket space, those who put ample thought into their appearance and its implications, those for whom cargo shorts have become a symbol of ambivalence and laziness, and those who surround themselves with men for whom cargo shorts are an insult and affront, see them as the absolute bottom of the sartorial barrel.

Based on which camp you lean toward you're probably either agreeing with the first assessment or the second and think the opposing group is wrong.

But what if both are right?

Appearance, unlike morality, isn't about right or wrong, it's about effective vs ineffective. It's about being able to have the way you look enhance your life.

That improvement may come from dressing in a suit and tie, but if you're working in a coal mine, a bespoke jacket from a tailoring house in London is probably an ineffective choice for you. Just as much as the man who wants to teach at an elementary school will probably be more hurt than helped if he's covered in tattoos from head to toe.

There's no such thing as a good appearance - especially when we live in a global society in which major things like right and wrong can't be universally agreed upon. Yes beauty has its roots in nature, math, and symmetry and we'll touch on that in Chapter 6. But the manifestation of what is aesthetically pleasing isn't limited to one particular clothing style.

What may be completely awful for one group of people is entirely appropriate for another.

Rather than staying within the limiting mindset of good or bad, you need to adapt your approach and start seeing things like the clothes you wear, your grooming, your posture, and your other visual cues as amoral tools that are either helping you in life or hurting you in life.

Here's an example - part of my daily routine is to check the stats, comments, and referral links on my various social media and writing platforms.

Every once in a while, my main site - Masculine Style - will experience a boost in traffic that invariably comes from an article or video of mine being posted to an online forum - typically geared specifically towards men. And, unless that forum is specific to men's clothing and appearance, the threads almost always look the same.

It goes something like this:

- Original Post - Here's a reason you should dress better

- One group of commenters - We agree, here are a bunch of links to different people who can teach you how to dress better

- Second group of commenters - This is a stupid thread and proof of how much this entire forum has gone downhill over the last few weeks/months/years. A real man doesn't care what anyone else thinks of him and wears whatever he wants. Caring about clothing is stupid/effeminate/gay/frivolous. Defense of decision to wear cargo shorts, combat boots, and T-shirts with logos.

- First group of commenters - It's not stupid/effeminate/gay/frivolous, it's a way to show self-respect and get ahead in life.

- Second group - all that matters is hard work. The only priority of clothing should be function. Here is anecdotal evidence of why dressing better doesn't help them in their lives.

- First group - It would still improve your life if you decided to give it a try. Here's a link.

- Second group - no it won't. You're ridiculous. The guy who wrote that article you're linked to is stupid and in no way masculine.

And on and on and on for twice or three times the number of pages as the average thread gets.

Now, I'm willing to admit that my own experience with this may be entirely anecdotal, but I've both seen this play out and had it pointed out to me by others often enough, that I'm more and more willing to recognize it as an actual trend.

The irony is that both sides are engaging in a hotly contested discussion in which one of the parties continually tries to affirm to itself and to its opponent that even discussing the matter is in conflict with its identity.

This puzzled me for years until I realized that all men have a relationship with clothing. We'll talk later about how we men use our appearances to communicate our masculine traits and virtues to the rest of the world, but first we need to establish the relationship men have with the way we look.

Why is it that some men are willing to dress better and exhort others to do so, while others are so opposed to the idea they'll exert disproportionate amounts of energy in an attempt to convince their peers of the drawbacks and downsides of caring about clothing?

Why is it that those who have an entirely negative relationship with clothing almost always dress the same and look like each other? Does mankind have an aesthetic, lowest common denominator toward which we'll all fall once we decide we don't care about the image we project?

If function is the top priority of these men and their relationship with their clothing, then why don't they all wear amorphous jumpsuits or coveralls all day?

Have men always felt this way about their clothing, grooming, and appearance, or is this a relatively recent phenomenon? Does this attitude only (or largely) occur in Western cultures or is it something that can be found throughout the world and across history?

After pondering and writing on these questions for years, I've identified two principles.

1. All men care about our appearance.

2. The level to which we care is proportionate to the value we get from doing so.

Let me explain.

There are three types of relationships a man can have with the concept of clothing and appearance - antipathy, neutrality, or affinity. The lines between these are blurry and the same man can find himself somewhere in between two of the different attitudes or even fully experience all three in different environments.

The antipathy attitude is one that has taken hold in the West in the past 60 years and is the dominant mindset amongst those who concern themselves with the ideas of masculinity and what it means to be a good man.

To these men, the concern for one's appearance is so antithetical to true and traditional masculinity that the expression of this concern becomes an immediate disqualification.

"You care about how you look? You can't be a real man."

For these men, the only appropriate masculine relationship to clothing is seeing it as a necessary evil that has one redeeming quality - function.

Any concern for clothing, beyond how little you paid for it, how comfortable it is, and how it can help you in the pursuit of other acceptable masculine goals, is a sign of effeminacy and grounds to write off your manhood.

Even though those with an antipathy mindset have the loudest voice, there's a relatively low number of men who actually feel this way. The vast majority of individuals fall more into the realm of neutrality.

The neutrality attitude can be summed up like this - "As long as I don't look bad, I don't really care how I look."

I believe that this is the typical modern Western man's approach to clothing. He has things he refuses to wear and possibly a favorite shirt or pair of shoes - but most of his concern with clothing is neutral or indifferent.

He'll wear a suit and tie when he needs to, but he doesn't look great. His casual clothing doesn't look terrible on him - at least not to the point where he looks like he's given up on life. He doesn't stand out, nor does he evoke any sort of emotional response. He doesn't impress anyone, but he doesn't ostracize anyone either.

His wife may not love the way he dresses, but she's not secretly hiding or donating his bad clothing because she's embarrassed to be seen with him. His kids, friends, co-workers, and employers never really think about what he's wearing because it's as neutral as what nearly every other man is wearing.

He sees better dressed men and casually thinks, "That looks great, but it's not for me." or, "I wonder what I'd look like if I dressed like that," but then he lets the thought process stop there.

If this describes you, it's natural to think that you arrived at this attitude organically and without any effort. That may be true, but it doesn't mean your relationship with your clothing is any less part of your identity as both the man who resents anyone who considers dressing well and the one who gets dressed with care each day.

If you doubt this, then I challenge you to dress either up or down one or two levels in formality from what you and the people around you are used to you wearing. If you're hesitant or completely unwilling to do this, think about why. What is it that holds you back? How do you rationalize the decision in your head?

If you are willing to try this, pay attention to how you feel and act when you're dressed differently. How do other people treat you? How do you respond to the way they're treating you? How do you see yourself?

Why is it that your life can be so different from just the simple act of either dressing better or worse than how you (and the rest of your social circle) currently dress?

It's because you, and your in-group, have carefully cultivated a standard of acceptable appearance and you're content to remain within the neutral zone.

At this point, you may be thinking that I'm making some sort of moral judgment about your character or your convictions. And this is the furthest thing from the truth. Some of the most successful, driven, powerful men in the world have had a neutral relationship with their clothing.

I'm not suggesting that these particular men would have been or can be more successful if they dress better. I believe these few are so driven and dedicated, so willing to take risks and make sacrifices, that they would be successful with or without their attitude about clothing.

And even without it affecting their business success, does their appearance not impact their relationships with others, their self perception, or their evolution into the next phase in their lives?

What I *am* suggesting however, is if you're not as driven and dedicated, and not as willing to take risks and make sacrifices, then improving your appearance can help you attain more success in life.

Facebook's CEO - Mark Zuckerburg - is notorious for his bad clothing choices - simple T-shirts, poorly fitting jeans, and slip-on sandals that are better suited for the gym locker room than the board room. Zuckerburg didn't accomplish what he did with Facebook because of his style, but in spite of it.

When asked about his wardrobe he talks about freeing up mental energy by choosing a uniform (more on that in chapter 10). What's interesting though, is that his uniform wouldn't require any more or less mental energy if it consisted of a three-piece suit, a dress, or a mechanic's coverall.

He's landed on the clothing he's chosen not only because it's easy for him to get dressed each morning, but because those particular items are communicating to him and those around him that he's aesthetically neutral. But if he were to run in different social circles, if his success were more dependent on having an affinity for his appearance, he likely would dress very differently.

The affinity attitude is the rarest and also has the strongest level of variation. Affinity for dressing well can be as simple as taking pride in what you wear and as complicated as having your life revolve around and cater entirely to your appearance.

There have been men with aesthetic affinity in all cultures and throughout history. It is this attitude that causes men to take pride wearing their team jersey or dress uniform. It is the approach that makes the green jacket of the Masters and the white coat of a doctor valuable statements of achievement, accomplishment, and authority. It is the attitude that leads little boys to "dress up" like their favorite super heroes in their attempts to emulate them in as many ways as possible.

But affinity also has its positives and its negatives. A healthy affinity for appearance is a willingness to see it and embrace it as the amoral tool that it is. It is an ability and willingness to cultivate an appearance that contributes toward success in more important endeavors. It sees appearance as the ability to externally express who you are internally and use that expression to improve your life and the lives of those around you.

An unhealthy affinity for appearance is an obsession with looks, the placement of appearance as the highest priority and the driving factor of each decision, and the conflation of value between how you look and who you are. It sees appearance as the ability to internally create who you are by basing your identity off of what the rest of the world wants you to be. It conflates expression with creation and makes your identity something that is defined by others, rather than yourself.

Understandably, most men want to avoid developing an obsession with our appearance, sometimes for the right reasons - like recognizing that appearance is not as important as substance, wanting to avoid drawing too much attention, and a resistance to the social risk that can come from dressing too differently from peers.

Sometimes though, it's for the wrong reasons - like the belief that any obvious or expressed concern for appearance is shallow, vapid, or only appropriate for women.

Many men will subconsciously fear that any intentional efforts toward improving their appearance will lead them down a path to becoming a metrosexual diva - as if the only protection from becoming image obsessed is to avoid any concern for appearance whatsoever.

It's how many of us are wired. We believe if we're going to do anything, we'll take it to its extreme.

In his prime, the legendary bodybuilder Arnold Schwarzenegger would dwarf his competition and absolutely tower over average people. He would often find himself in conversations with different men who would ultimately say something along the line of, "I never want to look like you."

In response, and true to form, Schwarzenegger had a one-liner that hit hard and accurately:

"You never will"

It's a common thought for men who start lifting weight or getting into better shape to think, "I don't want to get too big" or "I don't want to look too bulky" as if that will somehow sneak up on them. One day they'll go to bed a normal, healthy-looking man, and the next morning they'll wake up with an additional 50 pounds of muscle and the inability to comfortably rest their arms at their sides.

It's obviously a silly fear and one which trainers and nutrition coaches quickly disabuse for their clients. The men who look like Schwarzenegger didn't arrive there haphazardly or by accident. It required years of work, dedication, and sacrifice.

If you find yourself wanting a more positive relationship with your appearance, but are worried doing so will mean you'll be having plastic surgery, laser hair removal, and regular manicures in five years, you're falling into the same mental trap as the men new to weight lifting.

You won't go to bed one night with a authentic, intentional, masculine wardrobe and wake up the next morning as a dandy who can't leave the house because the rain will ruin his suede opera pumps - not unless you want to get to.

But, recognizing your own relationship with clothing is only half the battle.

If you were the only person affected by what you chose to wear, it would be easy to dress well. You could focus entirely on what your clothing did for you - in how it functioned and how it made you feel - and leave it at that.

However one of the major, if not primary, reasons your appearance matters is because of how it affects your relationships with other people around you.

I know what you're probably thinking at this point. It's something along the lines of either "I don't care what anyone else thinks of me," or, "I shouldn't care what anyone else thinks of me."

It's an odd tenet of the modern twist on masculinity and one that deserves to be completely eradicated.

If you do find yourself thinking this way, I want you to picture the four most important men in your life. Maybe it's your best-friend from high school whom you still have contact with, a mentor, your co-worker, your dad, your brothers, or your son. It doesn't matter who it is, just think of the four most important men in your life.

Now think about whether their opinion of you really matters. Are they loyal to you and are you loyal to them? Is there some semblance of honor, respect, and expectation between you? Or can you simply think, say, and do whatever you want without it ever having any sort of negative impact on those relationships?

If all of those men were to come to you today and tell you they despised you, you've lost their trust, and you have no business being associated with them anymore, do you believe their saying so would have absolutely no effect on you?

Odds are, probably not. And that's a great thing! Virtues like honor and loyalty are essential components of masculinity and are what make human civilizations function.

Should you have the same response if a random stranger approached you on the street and told you he despised you, didn't trust you, and had no loyalty to you? Of course not!

And this is where the confusion comes in. Just because you shouldn't be overly affected by what a stranger or acquaintance thinks of you doesn't mean you should not care what anyone thinks.

Once you realize that the opinions of the people close to you both do and should matter, it becomes easier to align your attitudes and actions to maintain that in-group loyalty.

I believe you should do what is right, irrespective of what anyone, either in or outside of your group thinks of you, but once you've left the realm of right vs wrong, the impact of your actions on your tribe should be considered when making decisions.

And this is where the importance of appearance matters. If everyone in your community decides to wear red shirts and you show up in blue - you signal a separation from that community and impact your relationship with those people. You may want to assimilate and wear red, or rebel and wear blue. That's up to you and you should choose accordingly. But, it's foolish to wish to rebel and wear red, or wish to conform and wear blue.

Obviously rebellion and assimilation, aspiration and contentment, loyalty and disloyalty are defined by actions, ideas, and decisions infinitely more important than the color of your shirt. But your appearance serves as a primary way to signal, both to yourself and to other people, if you want to assimilate, aspire, or rebel.

The impact appearance has isn't limited to simple in-group or ex-group signaling. It goes beyond that into the realm of morality.

It is often difficult for people to separate "what I'm used to" from "what is right" and we can easily fall into the trap of distinguishing attributes like the morality of other men by what they choose or don't choose to wear.

Your appearance doesn't determine your character. However it does help reinforce it within your own self perception and communicate it to the world around you though.

You may be thinking it's shallow, unfair, or even immoral for you to try to determine the character of other people based on their appearance. Our world tells us not to judge a book by its cover.

That's a well-meaning but impossible task. The better approach is judge and then be willing to give that book a chance to prove the initial judgment right or wrong, irrespective of its cover.

A man in your community may be loyal and wear blue, or be a rebel who wears red. That doesn't make your initial assessment of him immoral or entirely erroneous. It just means you didn't have enough information, based on his appearance alone, to make an accurate judgment. You start from what his clothing, grooming, body language, and facial expressions tell you, then either reassess or double down if other information confirms or denies those initial judgments.

Not only is it not immoral for us to make decisions about people based on their appearance, it's biologically programmed into us.

If we were to try to avoid making quick judgments based on perceived patterns of behavior, our brains would quickly become overwhelmed and shut down.

As I'm typing this I'm sitting on an airplane. While paying attention to the people around me, I've used visual cues like their body language, posture, clothing, and facial expressions to help determine how I should respond to them.

From a survival standpoint, the safest assumption is that every other person on this plane poses a threat and needs to be treated accordingly. But there are mental and psychological costs for operating with this as an omnipresent belief.

Instead, my mind subconsciously scans the people around me for any perceived signals of a threat. Things like sex, age, gender, size, style, and behavior are all preprogramed stimuli our brains use to help us determine who's a threat, who's neutral and who's a friend.

Of course these cues and classifications can be wrong, but they're always going on in the background. It's up to us to use the conscious, intentional parts of our brain to override or adhere to the signals we're picking up on from everyone around us.

And doing so requires more work than you might think.

There is a term used in ethology (the study of animal behavior) called Fixed Action Patterns. These are set behavior sequences that occur automatically when an animal receives a particular stimulus.

For example, there is a type of diving beetle that uses the angle of the sun to help ensure it swims along the water's surface. By maintaining a perfect 90 degree angle, it doesn't dive any deeper than it intends to.

These same beetles have been "tricked" into swimming upside down by placing them in an aquarium and lighting it from below.

Their biological programming tells them where the "sun" is and their fixed action programming engages, flipping the body over and causing them to swim upside down

We may think the animal is silly or undeveloped because it is incapable of using other features like its sight, equilibrium, and intelligence to determine when it is swimming upside down, but we shouldn't be too quick to write it off as a simple creature.

Humans are equally subject to the same types of automated responses to certain stimuli.

And, as you can imagine, clothing is one stimulus that can have a huge impact on how people behave. Not only does our appearance affect the way other people perceive, treat, and interact with us, it also alters how we feel about ourselves.

To properly illustrate these effects, let's talk about one particular piece of clothing that is infused with meaning in Western culture - the white coat.

In 2012, Northwestern University scholars Hajo Adam and Adam Galinsky, conducted an experiment attempting to answer a question - could wearing clothing that has specific and symbolic meaning affect the wearer's thoughts and emotions?

In order to test their thesis, they conducted experiments using a lab coat. Their hypothesis was that a white lab coat - a garment used to convey authority, discipline, intelligence, and focus - would lead to test subjects feeling more authoritative, disciplined, intelligent, and focused when worn.

One round of experiments was used to test the idea that a white coat can mean different things to different people and therefore have varied impacts on their behavior.

In the experiment 99 undergraduate students were selected to take a test gauging their ability to detect minor differences between two nearly identical pictures, placed side-by-side.

One third of the students were told the white jacket was a medical doctor's coat and were told to put it on. Another third was also instructed to wear the jacket but were told it was the kind worn by an artist to protect his clothing from paint. The final third had the jacket placed in front of them and were told it was a doctor's lab coat.

Each of the subjects was asked to write a quick essay about what meaning the coat had for them.

All were then tested on their ability to identify the variations between a set of pictures placed in front of them. They were instructed to write down the differences as quickly as possible.

Because all participants took about the same time to complete the test, persistence was ruled out as a potential factor in the different results the researchers found.

Upon studying the data, they discovered that those who were told they were wearing a doctor's coat identified more differences than those who believed they were wearing a painter's smock. Those who looked at the doctor's coat but didn't actually wear it scored between the two groups.

"The main conclusion that we can draw from the studies is that the influence of wearing a piece of clothing depends on both its symbolic meaning and the physical experience of wearing the clothes," Adam and Galinsky said.

Those who both wore the jacket and identified it as a doctor's coat were able to better focus their minds as a result of wearing the garment.

Adam and Galinksy labeled the effect "Enclothed Cognition" and it can be seen in soldiers and athletes wearing uniforms, businessmen wearing suits, and myriad other instances wherein particular pieces of clothing have strong symbolism.

So, let's take this whole idea of Enclothed Cognition, and how it can help our own perception of ourselves, and then add to it something called the Halo Effect.

The term Halo Effect originated in 1920 from psychologist Edward Thorndike in an article detailing confirmation biases and their causes.

Essentially the Halo Effect is the phenomenon in which one good quality spreads its appeal onto other characteristics of a person.

Think about it this way, you've recently moved to a new city and are looking to build some friendships. You head to a nearby bar and see two men sitting alone. Both are wearing the same clothes, drinking the same drink, and watching the same game. However, one is sitting up straight, smiling, and engaging the other people at the bar whereas the other is slouched, refusing to make eye contact, and has his jaw set.

Imagine having the exact same word-for-word conversation with both men. However, don't imagine it being engaging and fun, but awkward, a bit difficult to get through, and ultimately unfulfilling.

Because of the Halo Effect your brain will handle the awkwardness of that conversation with each man a little differently. With the charismatic, confident man you may simply think that you two just didn't connect or worse, you were the difficult one and the reason things got awkward. You'd most likely walk away from that conversation still liking him and wishing it had gone better. His good characteristics of confidence and charisma override the negative experience of an awkward, forced conversation.

On the other hand, you'll consider the second man as the source of the conversation's difficulty and walk away thinking he's a weird loser and not someone with whom you want to be friends.

Same conversation - different perspectives all because of the minor tweak in body language.

The Halo Effect can be applied with any positive character trait - from the way we smell, to the positive things other people say about us, to the way we dress.

In fact, clothing and appearance are huge components of the Halo Effect. Those who are considered to be more attractive are typically, "Better liked, more persuasive, more frequently helped, and seen as possessing more desirable personality traits and greater intellectual capacity."

Pairing Enclothed Cognition with the Halo Effect is an incredibly powerful 1-2 punch that can very easily set you up for success - especially because they can have a synergistic effect on each other.

The stronger your own self confidence is, the more it comes across to other people. And the more other people see you as confident and capable, the more they like you. The more they like you and treat you with respect, the more you increase in confidence. And on and on it goes.

Now obviously improving your appearance does not create competence out of thin air. Putting on a white lab coat does not give you the understanding and dexterity of a doctor - it just helps you better access information that's already in your brain.

And dressing well and having good body language won't make up for being socially incompetent, morally corrupt, or emotionally stunted.

Even with the help of the Halo Effect, one positive trait can't outweigh a host of negatives.

But appearance does matter and you can improve your life by improving your style, as long as the changes you're making are actual improvements. After all, dressing well isn't a one-size-fits-all approach.

3 POWER VS APPEAL

Too many men hear "dress well" and interpret it as "look nice/good/pretty."

They see the women in their lives spend time focusing on their clothing, grooming, and overall appearance and assume that the pursuit of looking good or dressing well is inherently feminine.

As I've spoken to men in different conferences and events, one of the most common things I've heard is, "My wife picks all my clothes for me." or, "My mom used to dress me and I never really thought about it after that." or, "I hate shopping and just wear what my girlfriend thinks I look good in."

Nine times out of ten I don't need these men to tell me that's the case, because I can tell just from looking at them.

When a woman dresses herself, her primary goal is visual appeal. She wants to accentuate the things that make her beautiful and this desire is driven by a few different components.

Human beings are sexually dimorphic creatures - which basically means that men and women are biologically different. Because we're different, we have distinct priorities and unique ways of making ourselves valuable to other people - both in looking for a mate and in looking for status or a position within a group or society.

Biologically and historically, women have been able to find both their place within the group and their ideal mate by being the most fertile and the most capable of creating the strongest, most-likely-to-survive offspring. It's only within the past hundred or so years that society, technology, and culture have created an environment in which women are able to work alongside men and choose to embrace, delay, or eschew altogether their biological drive to have children.

Culture and human behavior take that biological priority and amplify it. Men seek the most beautiful women we can find - either to be with or at least surround ourselves with. Not only do we love being around attractive women, but we know that it's higher status men who are able to attract the most appealing partners. A woman's beauty becomes a subconscious way for men to jockey for position and status amongst ourselves. In black-and-white terms, we believe the best man gets the hottest girl.

And don't think it's just men who take advantage of this. Women are just as status anxious as we are and know their position within the social hierarchy of a given group depends largely on how attractive they can be. In fact, more often than not, women are dressing not for the men in their lives, but to compete with and outrank the other women in their group.

So the value of a woman's attractiveness starts with a biological drive and signal, is added to by how that applies to men and our status, and is capped off by how it raises or lowers a woman's own status. Essentially beauty, attractiveness and visual appeal are a huge component of a woman's success - whether she likes it or not.

The naturally beautiful embrace this and do everything they can to give themselves a competitive edge. The rest may choose to do everything they can to look as beautiful as possible, or simply decry the value of beauty altogether and embrace social movements that try to minimize the importance of physical appeal.

Either way - whether a woman "leans in" to the idea that beauty matters, or spends hundreds of hours writing online screeds to the contrary - they both know that it does have a strong place in our current society.

As men, our value to the group and our ability to attract the best women is not dependent on how physically attractive we appear. Yes there are still biological markers of genetic fitness - things like a strong jaw signaling higher levels of testosterone or broad shoulders that imply more strength - but the value in our appearance is almost entirely related to how it signals our utility.

When a woman dresses well, what does she do?

She maximizes her femininity - even if it happens subconsciously. Heels change her posture so her chest sticks out, her calves look bigger, and her legs appear longer. Mascara and eye shadow make the eyes larger, tipping the balance of the face to an appearance that's more feminine, innocent, and appealing. Following the latest trend projects youth and status.

When taken to its extreme, it's fairly obvious that men and women have different aesthetic goals. It's why our clothing is made differently and most people avoid anything that's either clearly made for the opposite sex or is even too androgynous.

But once the water gets a little muddy, once we start to think the end goal of dressing well is something as vague and ethereal as "looking good" then it's more difficult to identify how to accomplish that goal.

This problem is compounded by two simple assumptions: 1. Men don't know or care how to dress well and 2. Women do.

Now, both of these stereotypes exist for good reason, but that doesn't mean that the solution is to ask the important women in your life for style advice.

Let's go back to another exercise analogy. If you're carrying around some extra pounds, get winded easily, and generally don't like the way you feel, you decide you want to get in shape - a goal that involves diet and exercise.

If you want to lose the gut and put on more muscle, you're going to start seeking advice from someone who lifts weights. If you want to simply slim down - get lean and not worry about putting on any size, you'll turn to someone like a marathon runner for advice.

Both the bodybuilder and the long-distance runner are in better shape than you are, but both took very different paths to get there. If you want to look, feel, and perform like the marathoner, you don't want to take nutrition and exercise advice from the bodybuilder and vice versa.

Both athletes have different goals and use different means to accomplish those ends.

So unless you want to dress like the women in your life, getting their style advice will often do more damage than good.

Rather than helping you look more established, credible, authoritative, and powerful they'll choose clothing that makes you appear younger, trendier, more beauty oriented, and more feminine.

Which is a problem for the average man because - just as a woman's highest sexual market value is demonstrated through signals of fertility, youth, and beauty - a man's is shown through usefulness, bravery, and power.

In fact, youth and beauty are both liabilities for men as both imply a lack of interaction with the outside world, an inability to provide and protect, and an untested potential that leaves your worth unknown.

While the primary aesthetic goal for women is visual appeal, the main objective for men is visual power.

Now, don't think that the means to accomplishing those disparate ends have to be entirely different.

Let's take one of the most feminine components of beauty as an example - makeup.

While there is a movement amongst modern, androgynous, males to start embracing makeup and feminine beauty standards, the vast majority of us wouldn't be caught dead putting on foundation or a little eye shadow in the morning. From both our cultural conditioning and biological imperatives, we know that making our eyes appear more feminine becomes an aesthetic negative rather than a positive. And, when we do see men who have made the jump over to wearing makeup in the same manner as women, it makes most of us uncomfortable.

That said, some of the most powerful men in the world will have makeup applied every day. It may be actors on a set or politicians before going live on the news, but these movers and shakers in society are often having powder applied to their faces to avoid shine from the lights and the camera.

Do we see this as inherently negative? No because we understand that the application of makeup is used as a neutralizer. The goal of the powder is not to enhance certain characteristics, it's to compensate for what the camera does and get the wearer back to a state of neutrality.

The goal of makeup on a news anchor is not to make him look more appealing. It's to make him look normal.

But, we can continue to take the concept further. Because, it's not just getting back to neutral that can take something as feminine as makeup and make it acceptable.

There are many cultures in which the application of paint on the face and body was inherently masculine.

Native American tribes, Scottish rebels, African warriors, and many other cultures have used paint as a way to communicate visual power, signal status, strike fear into the hearts of their enemies, and mark acts of bravery.

The body and face paint don't have any inherent or biological meaning to them. However, by assigning value to the markings, they become potent tools for the men wearing them to signal their power to others.

A man who's dressed and made up in a feminine way may be much more capable of killing me than one who's in a loin cloth and covered in body paint but I know which one I'd fear encountering more, and it's all because the first is communicating beauty and the second is signaling power.

But direct, violent power isn't the only kind of strength available to men. If that were the case history would be full of leaders who were physically strong, violent, and dominant.

Power can be wielded (and communicated) indirectly as well. For example, let's talk about the peruke.

That word may be unfamiliar but it's the name of an item that is known all too well - a powdered wig.

In the late 16th century the plague of syphilis was rampant in Europe. And, because of a lack of modern medicinal practices we take for granted today, those who contracted the STD took the brunt of it. Open sores, dementia, rashes, hair loss, and even blindness were all common symptoms of the disease and were experienced by many.

During this time long hair was a status symbol and baldness was a sure-fire way to be ostracized from polite society. To protect themselves from immediate damage to their reputation, syphilis-ridden men took to wearing wigs of goat, horse, or even human hair. However, while this saved many of them from becoming outcasts, the wigs themselves were obvious cover-ups for a natural problem - not a display of status on their own.

At least, that was the case until 1655 when the king of France began to lose his hair. Louis XIV was at a ripe old age of only 17 when his balding started to become apparent and, rather than lose face, he hired four dozen wigmakers to alleviate his problem. Five years later, the king of England did the same thing once his hair started to grey.

Because of the power - both physical and social - that these kings wielded, the aristocracy began to adopt the trend of wearing wigs. And, as trends are prone to do, perukes trickled down to the upper-middle class and became the latest fad in Europe.

The price and size of wigs rose drastically. Large, envy-inducing perukes sold for 32 times what the average wig went for and the term "bigwig" became synonymous with power and authority and is still used today.

What was initially a less-than-effective way for an unfortunate balding fellow to retain his status quickly became one of the most coveted and expensive accoutrements a man could acquire - all because it conveyed a message of financial and social power.

These wigs displayed zero direct power. They weren't symbols of men slain in battle, nations conquered, or lands discovered. Instead they represented indirect, social and financial power.

Like many displays of wealth and status, perukes communicated to the lower and working classes that those who wore them were above menial labor, could afford ostentatious displays of wealth, and didn't have to rely on their own direct sources of power to affect the world around them.

While the modern West, especially countries like the United States, may seemingly reject such displays of conspicuous consumption - we still see luxury vehicles, designer-brand clothing, uncalloused hands, and other displays of indirect power from men today.

Which all comes back to the ancient, biological underpinnings of what it takes to be an effective man. Power is the confidence and competence necessary to take on risk and turn it into reward. Power is how men have fulfilled our traditional roles to provide, protect, preside, and procreate. Power is what protected us and our families from the saber-tooth tigers and men from other tribes who wanted to take our resources for their own.

While most men today won't confront a whole lot of physical danger, we do have our own ways of facing risk and exemplifying power. In fact, there are plenty of men who would feel more comfortable in a fist fight than approaching a woman at a bar.

Because, even though physical risk has largely been outsourced to other men, social risk is still something every one of us has to grapple with each and every day.

Do you play it safe and not talk to anyone you don't already know but then miss out on the opportunities that can come from expanding your social circle?

Do you open yourself up to meeting new people and deepening your network but also risk exposing yourself to rejection and watching that rejection snowball into outright repulsion from polite society?

Do you stand out in a sea of blue shirts and wear red because you're willing to identify with a different culture or simply reject the status quo around you?

Do you blend in and wear blue because doing so means you aren't worrying about the drawbacks and costs that come from standing out and can be free to focus on other ways to accomplish your goals?

These are all questions with which we wrestle, albeit subconsciously for most of us. They are problems we are confronted by and trade offs we're expected to make.

For many men, the ability to take and overcome social risks is one of the biggest advantages they have.

While direct power may be more easily communicated universally - a warrior covered in scars wearing a necklace of human ears is going to be intimidating regardless of where you're from - indirect power is much more context dependent.

For example, something that is seen as a "universal" standard of power today - the well-made business suit, doesn't translate to all subcultures within Western civilization. Try wearing a suit to a meeting for a startup or into an MMA gym and see how far it gets you.

Nor does its power translate into other non-Western cultures. A man who is part of a small tribe in the Amazon who's never had contact with the outside world will not be impressed by a suit. Any man wearing one there will look odd and ridiculous.

And even within established, Western culture, the suit's symbol of indirect power doesn't span all time. It doesn't matter how well made a double-breasted, Tom Ford, charcoal suit is - if it's being worn to a meeting with the Sons of Liberty during the American revolution, it's going to look out of place and inconsistent with any mode of influence and status at the time.

Thankfully a lack of universalism doesn't make something impossible to understand - especially because most masculine communication, whether direct or indirect, falls within a few key virtues that do exist across both time and culture.

4 MASCULINITY & AESTHETICS

We've already talked about the difference between men and women and how aesthetics help each accomplish different goals.

However, in order to truly communicate your masculinity through your appearance, we need to identify what it means to be a man.

It's a question that has been pondered and discussed for ages. And, while there are many ideas and philosophies available, I believe the best, most succinct answer, has been put out by author Jack Donovan in his title *The Way of Men*.

In this book, Donovan makes a key and important distinction that is critical to understanding masculinity. Because of Christian and other religious influences, the modern world is either incapable or unwilling to see masculinity as amoral - meaning it is difficult for us to separate whether a man is good or bad from whether he is masculine or not.

For most the focus is either heavily on what it means to be a good man, or they believe that masculinity, and its focus, are inherently outdated, closed-minded, or even evil. Those who favor traditional masculinity will often argue against holding any immoral man up as an example of effective manliness. Whereas those who resent traditional gender roles have increasingly seen any and all masculinity as toxic, dangerous, and indicative of a bad person.

If you were to poll your immediate social circle and ask them what it is that makes a male a good man, the odds are in favor of their giving responses that are equally applicable to both men and women. Things like honesty, hard work, self sufficiency, integrity, and concern for the well being of others are excellent answers when defining a good person, but they ring hollow when attempting to differentiate between a man and a woman or a man and a child.

Morality and all of its practices are not limited to men or even to adults. Yet sadly, most people will stop here in their attempts to define a good man.

A few will pick up the torch and seek to look a little deeper. For the most part, their answers will come in negative statements. A man doesn't cry. A man doesn't take advantage of those who are weaker than him. A man isn't soft or a sissy.

While these may be equally true, there is a problem when masculinity is only defined by the actions we choose to omit. And, while eschewing certain behaviors has always been an important aspect of defining manhood, it is now the only politically correct and socially safe way in which masculinity can be considered in the modern, Western world.

By taking the positive power, the things a man does (as opposed to only the things he refuses to do) out of the working definition of what it is to be a man, our modern world has denied masculinity its teeth, its authority, and its power.

Unfortunately the average man no longer associates positive, committed action with the definition of manhood.

However, Donovan separates masculinity from good or evil by simply approaching it this way - there is a difference between being a good man and being good at being a man.

We all know men who are good people but whom we'd struggle to define as masculine. Just like we all know (or are at least aware of) men who typify masculinity incredibly well, but can't be defined as good or virtuous people.

Once we know that masculinity and goodness don't have a direct correlation, it becomes easier to look at what makes a man good at being a man.

Donovan labels these characteristics as the Four Tactical Virtues and defines them as follows:

- Courage

- Strength

- Mastery

- Honor

A possession, internalization, and demonstration of each of these virtues is essential to being good at being a man. And, as you can imagine, these four virtues are very strongly caught up in the aesthetic decisions men have made throughout the ages.

Courage

Whether it's hunting large beasts or protecting against invaders, courage has been a core component of masculinity from our inception. And masculine cultures have always found ways to reward, support, and canonize courageous men.

Because courage - be it physical, moral, social, or any other form - is so vital to masculinity, and because it's always been a way by which we measure ourselves against our peers, it is only logical that men would find ways to signal our courage through clothing and appearance.

From gang tattoos, to tribal totems, to medals awarded in the military, courageous men have long benefitted from the demonstration and reaffirmation of their courageous acts through clothing and other visual symbolism.

During the late 19th and early 20th centuries, upper-class university students in Austria and Germany developed a particular fondness for Mensur - academic fencing.

Fraternal fencing organizations had existed for centuries before, but during this particular time period, they experienced a strong resurgence. The individual duels had a ritualistic feel and, in many cases, varying levels of protection - eye, nose, chest, etc. - were worn.

However, rather than wanting full protection and avoiding all damage, many of the young men intentionally sought facial cuts and their subsequent scars.

These wounds, known as Schmisse, were a badge of honor, status, and courage and were highly regarded by both the young men in these fraternities and the women they were interested in. So much so that bearing a Schmisse was evidence of a man being "good husband material"

The scars were so popular that some men took to cutting themselves with razors or paying doctors to cut their cheeks for them. But, because this was clearly disassociated from participation in a duel, these scars were not just ignored but outright rejected as dishonorable. These young men adopted an unearned symbol of courage and were rightly shunned for doing so.

The aesthetic power of the Schmisse did not come from any sort of beauty or symmetry but from what it represented - a willingness to engage in bladed combat, with a worthy foe, and to face that challenge with bravery and resolve. The same scar - if received from an accident or through some other means - would never be as powerful because it did not tell a story of courage, only misfortune.

But the relationship between clothing and courage isn't only intended to demonstrate the resolve and power of the wearer, it can just as effectively be used to discourage the perceiver.

One of the best examples of using his appearance to sap up the will and bravery of his opponents can be found in a man named Edward Teach - better known as Blackbeard the Pirate.

Six years after Blackbeard's death, Captain Charles Johnson published a pirate history and described Blackbeard as follows:

> Captain Teach assumed the cognomen [nickname] of Black-beard, from that large quantity of hair, which, like a frightful meteor, covered his whole face, and frightened America more than any comet that has appeared there in a long time.
> This beard was black, which he suffered to grow of an extravagant length; as to breadth, it came up to his eyes; he was accustomed to twist it with ribbons, in small tails … and turn them about his ears: in time of action, he wore a sling over his shoulders, with three brace of pistols, hanging in holsters like bandoliers [a belt worn over the shoulder]; and stuck lighted matches under his hat, which appearing on each side of his face, his eyes naturally looking fierce and wild, made him altogether such a figure, that imagination cannot form an idea of a fury, from Hell, to look more frightful.

Even his flag, which depicted a skeleton spearing a heart and raising a toast to the devil, was a visual tool to strike fear into the souls of those whom he attacked.

As terrifying and violent of a man as Teach was, he was also very practical. And he knew that the best and most effective way to win a battle was to get the opposing side to surrender before a single shot was ever fired.

Teach intentionally curated a horrific, demonic reputation and image for himself as a way to visually force others into submission and was successful in taking more than 40 ships during his short stint as a pirate. Many of these ships were given up without a fight simply because of the reputation and image of Blackbeard.

At this point you may be asking yourself what this has to do with you. After all, most of us find ourselves in the modern, civilized West and physical courage has largely become unnecessary, outsourced, or has to be intentionally sought out. How do the examples of Blackbeard and fencing club scars translate over to you?

Courage is a virtue necessary in contexts well beyond simply being willing to take a physical risk and can manifest itself in different forms. Yes the Schmisse and other historical examples are symbols of physical bravery, but there's much to be said for social courage and how it can be expressed through clothing.

Often cited as one of the most common fears, glossophobia - the fear of public speaking, is an intriguing example of a need for courage and can demonstrate an even greater phobia - the fear of embarrassment or public humiliation.

For most of us, there is no physical danger in speaking to a group of people. We don't worry that the microphone will explode, or even that the crowd will turn into a mob dead-set on burning us at the stake. What we fear is social rejection, embarrassment, and being ostracized from the group.

Many men will want to dismiss these fears as somehow less real or less important than those of physical danger or death. But, as we'll discuss in the chapter on Tribes, each man's standing within his own respective groups plays an important role in his health, wealth, happiness, and sanity.

Unlike physical danger and courage, social dangers change with culture and time. Jumping off of a cliff will always be dangerous, but wearing a particular article of clothing will have different results depending on the context in which it's worn. Take for example two different symbols of dominant ideologies - the Christian cross and the "=" of the equality movement.

Now, to make things more interesting, take their inverse - the inverted cross and a not equal "≠" and screen print both of those on a T-shirt.

In the United States in 1967, the inverted cross would require much more social courage to wear. Doing so could have cost you your job, relationships, and other opportunities. At the time, the dominant ideology was one that would see such a symbol as outright heresy and treat the wearer like a social leper. Which is why it was embraced by punk and other underground social movements.

While the consequences had become less severe, it can be argued that even as recently as 2007 there was still more social risk in wearing a symbol that rejected Christianity as opposed to one that defied equality.

But in the year 2017 having the audacity to wear or promote anything that contradicts the dominant ideology - that all people everywhere are equal - has much more serious ramifications and, therefore requires much more social courage than an anti-Christian symbol. Jobs have been lost and lives have been ruined as a result of men and women choosing to embrace the social risk that comes from symbols of counter cultures like the Alt Right and others.

Notice that social courage - much like masculinity - is amoral. It doesn't matter how you feel about either Christianity or Equality, any honest man will recognize that the social courage required to wear those particular symbols has shifted substantially over the past half a century.

Yet even beyond political statements and movements, social courage can be experienced and demonstrated in modern clothing.

We saw it in JFK when, as president, he chose to stop wearing a fedora and changed the Western world's relationship with the hat. We see it in teenagers who attend private school and rebel against the uniform by modifying or altering it. It's prevalent amongst the trend setters who are willing to wear something they know could just as equally lead to shame and ridicule as to fame or status. And we can even see it in the average man who decides he wants to improve himself and starts to dress a little more intentionally at the office. His coworkers often resent him for pointing out their own antipathy for a better appearance and can single him out for being willing to make himself better.

Social courage can be blatant or subtle, but it is something that can almost always be expressed through the clothing you choose to wear.

However, recognize that social risk will never be the same as having to face mortal peril. If you've inferred that public speaking or approaching an attractive woman at a bar requires the same type and level of courage as being on the front lines in war, you're mistaken.

And also note that social courage - just like physical - is not ignorance of the ramifications of one's actions. A man who picks a fight with a grizzly bear and doesn't understand the nature of the animal he's attacking isn't courageous, he's foolish. Just like a man headed to work sporting a mullet isn't necessarily showing any social courage if he doesn't understand that by doing so, he risks his standing amongst his peers.

Ignorance isn't courage in social situations any more than it is in physical scenarios.

Lastly, choosing to dress differently is an act of social courage in and of itself. If the expectation is casual and you knowingly arrive dressed formally, it required some level of social courage. And this doesn't just apply to formality. It can be equally effective in dressing more boldly, strongly, masterfully, or in any other way that separates you from the men around you.

Strength

Like courage, strength is vitally important in the physical realm, but can also be demonstrated beyond acts of the body.

Both the men and women of ancient Sparta dressed simply. After all, they were warriors first and laborers second, and their minimalistic approach to the other comforts of life crossed over into the clothing they wore.

When not in battle, their attire was simple, light, and functional. Even their battle attire was nearly identical to that of other Greek soldiers. However, when they were called to fight, their bland appearance was offset by one stark contrast - the color crimson.

The Spartans believed this deep red was the least feminine color and, therefore, best suited for the tasks of war. In addition to the masculine association, crimson had one very specific purpose - it minimized the appearance of blood.

Think of the psychological effect this small detail would have on a Spartan's enemies.

Even if an opponent felt his blade pierce the flesh of one of these soldiers, he wouldn't have visual confirmation. At the very least it would cause some doubt as to whether or not he'd made a clean hit. And, at its most effective, it would make the Spartan appear as if he were unaffected by the blows of his enemies.

This is clothing communicating strength at its most basic level. By simply making a tunic the color of blood, the wearer could be seen as impenetrable - making him a more formidable foe and having a massive impact on the morale of his enemies.

While the communication of strength to one's enemy has long been a tradition in warrior societies and classes, the relationship between strength and clothing can flow the other way as well.

Take for example the Eagle and Jaguar warriors of the Aztec Empire.

These were elite soldiers and entering their ranks was no simple task. Because captured enemies were used for ritualistic human sacrifices in religious ceremonies, it was much more valuable for a soldier to capture an enemy than to kill him on the battlefield. In fact, killing in battle was considered crude and unskilled by many Aztec soldiers.

In order to qualify to be an Eagle or Jaguar warrior a man had to capture four enemies in battle. And it is even believed by some historians that all four captures had to happen in a single battle to join the ranks.

Upon becoming a member of either elite society, these men had access to certain rights and privileges outside of war and were given an intense respect on the battlefield.

As a way to distinguish themselves both from other warriors and from each other, each society embraced a war costume that represented their chosen animals.

Eagle warriors were adorned in feathers and wore a helmet, shaped like an eagle, with their faces protruding from the beak. Their shields and weapons were also decorated with feathers and helped complete the ensemble.

Jaguar warriors wore the skins of jaguars and their head gear was made to look like the head of a jaguar, with their faces resting in the jaws.

Not only did this affect and weaken the courage of their enemies, but the warriors in these societies also believed, that by donning these particular war costumes, they would be given the strengths of the animals they represented.

These men understood the strengths of eagles and jaguars and wanted that power for themselves while engaged in battle. And they believed that their clothing would grant that to them.

We may not see that as overtly in the modern world (it's not like powerlifters wear the skins of buffalos or elephants in order to lift heavier weights), but we do see benefits from appearing stronger and larger - even in non-warrior societies.

This focus on strength is one of the reasons why the traditional suit has enjoyed such longevity as the epitome of modern style.

Unlike the hourglass figure that is considered ideal for a woman's body, we men look our best and strongest with a pronounced V-shape. At its most basic, the ideal male shape is one in which the shoulders are broader than the waist.

And this shape is exactly what the modern suit is designed to create - even if the man wearing it is far from a physical specimen of strength.

Broad shoulders, a narrow waist, and long lapels with an anchor point near the top of the chest or shoulders are all designed to make the shoulders look broader and the waist appear more narrow.

From a purely rational perspective, the man who looks more physically imposing may not be smarter, more qualified, or better suited (pun intended) for a given task, but our DNA runs deep and that Halo Effect we discussed earlier is very real. By looking stronger and more imposing, you will be given more deference, authority, respect, and admiration.

Mastery

If aesthetic signals of courage and strength seem to have become more subtle in the 21st century than in previous periods, the demonstration of mastery has only increased.

One of the most prominent and long lasting traditions of depicting mastery through clothing is alive and well today (albeit only in its ceremonial form) the academic regalia worn during graduation ceremonies.

These robes, and their accompanying symbolism, have been part of graduation ceremonies in universities for more than 800 years and have their roots in the religious symbolism that was part of the university climate at the time.

While that religious representation has long since left most universities, there is still a strong symbolic representation of mastery seen within the regalia.

The simplest distinction is that of the hood. According to the Academic Costume Code:

> ...the hood must be of the same material as the gown and its length is determined by the degree obtained.
> For a bachelor's degree the hood must be three feet, for the master's degree three and one-half feet, and for the doctor's degree, four feet. The hood worn for the doctor's degree only shall have panels at the sides.
> The hoods are to be lined with the official color or colors of the college or university conferring the degree; more than one color is shown by division of the field color in a variety of ways, chevron or chevrons, equal division, etc.
> The binding or edging of the hood is to be velvet or velveteen, two inches, three inches, and five inches wide for the bachelor's, master's, and doctor's degrees, respectively; the color should be indicative of the subject to which the degree pertains. For example, the trimming

> for the degree of Master of Science in Agriculture should be maize, representing agriculture, rather than golden yellow, representing science. No academic hood should ever have its border divided to represent more than a single degree.

So, not only does the length of the hood represent the level of mastery attained, but so does the width of the trimming.

As for trimmings on the gown,

> Gowns for the bachelor's and master's degrees are untrimmed. For the doctor's degree, the gown is faced down the front with black velvet; three bars of velvet are used to cross the sleeves. These facings and crossbars may be of velvet of the color distinctive of the disciplines to which the degree pertains; thus agreeing in color with the binding or edging of the hood appropriate to the particular doctor's degree in every instance.

Even the patterns with which the gowns are cut are used to distinguish between different levels of mastery within academia.

> The gown for the bachelor's degree has pointed sleeves. It is designed to be worn closed. The gown for the master's degree has an oblong sleeve, open at the wrist, like the others. The sleeve base hangs down in the traditional manner. The rear part of its oblong shape is square cut, and the front part has an arc cut away. The gown is so designed and supplied with fasteners that it may be worn open or closed. The gown for the doctor's degree has bell-shaped sleeves. It is so designed and supplied with fasteners that it may be worn open or closed.

But, even beyond the code there are long-standing traditions used to help distinguish different levels of mastery. For example, faculty and students may wear the same robes and have the same degrees, but faculty with doctoral degrees prefer wearing a velvet cap for both comfort and to distinguish themselves from the students.

Add to the above rules governing the wearing of tassels, stoles, and cords and it becomes easy to see how graduation regalia is centered around a demonstration of mastery and proficiency in the academic world.

But the visual depiction of mastery isn't limited to cultures with codified rules and hard hierarchies. It is prominent in almost any meritocratic culture or people.

To illustrate this, let me give you a personal example from my own life.

I have a brother who is 18 months younger than I am and he's practically a savant in the world of extreme sports. Whether it's winning trials competitions on a unicycle, mastering rails and skateparks on a scooter, or throwing himself with flips and twists off of a cliff in Southern Utah, my brother has always enjoyed seeing the limits to which he can push his body.

However, as much as he's enjoyed everything from golf to BMX, when we were in our teens and early 20's, his real passion was snowboarding.

And he's good - very good.

At the time he was most involved in the snowboard culture there was a particular trend going on in which pro and other riders would wear massive clothes and basketballs jerseys during the warm spring season.

Their pants sagged just the right amount, their goggles were cocked just so, and they all looked like they belonged to, and led, a very particular tribe.

Choosing to embrace this specific ensemble was a show of status and a way to tell the rest of the mountain that you were up and current on all the latest trends in the snowboarding world. However, because a snowboarder's worth in that culture is determined by his skillset and not by the clothes he wears, there was a huge amount of dissonance between communicating full immersion in the culture but not having the skills to back up that identity.

To put it more plainly - if you dressed like a pro snowboarder but rode like a beginner, it was obvious to everyone around you that you were a poser or, at the very least, just an incompetent rider.

At the same time, showing up on the mountain dressed like a skier, snowmobiler, or like you just got finished sledding was also a huge negative. You looked like you didn't belong to the culture at all and were treated like an outsider.

My brother was good enough that he could wear what all the other pros wore. While I, on the other hand, was left somewhere in the middle between looking like I was actually part of that world, but not so much that my lack of skill would contrast too starkly with the clothes I wore.

This same pattern can be seen in nearly any sport, hobby, or group of people. And while most people don't consciously recognize it and would refuse to address it, the majority of us are aware of the subtle style cues that denote mastery within our different worlds and where we fall within that hierarchy.

As you pay closer attention, you'll see markers of status and mastery in what's worn by men all around you - at work, at the gym, even a little league football game. Most of us play the mastery game subconsciously, and many of us play it only to the extent that we avoid looking socially incompetent, but we all play it.

Honor

If status within a particular group is tied to courage, strength, or mastery its worth comes from honor. And honor is one thing every masculine society lends toward.

Whether it's inner-city gangs, motorcycle clubs, ancient warrior societies, or a prison cell block - a masculine culture is one of honor, and one in which a man's standing with his peers (or enemies) is extremely important.

In the Democratic Republic of the Congo there is a group of people called the Salampasu. Surrounded by hostile neighbors, theirs is a warrior society and one that has a rigid hierarchy. The name is believed to mean "hunters of locusts" but they are feared and respected as fierce warriors by their neighboring tribes.

As a result, hunting and fighting are privileged occupations and not something to be treated lightly.

An integral component of this warrior society, and its associated status and hierarchy, is their use of masks.

They are made of wood and balls wound of reeds and are characterized by a bulbous forehead, a strong nose, pointed eyes, and a rectangular mouth filled with sharply pointed teeth. Masks that are used to represent leadership are covered by copper sheets.

The first mask is earned when a young boy is initiated into the society through a circumcision ritual. From there, he earns the right to additional masks via performing specific tasks and making large payments in livestock and other material possessions.

Upon becoming an owner of a particular mask, he is embraced by other owners and taught the particular knowledge associated with it.

Each mask's presentation matches a progressive order as the wearer moves up the ranks from hunter to warrior to chief.

Some masks are earned only through killing in battle, others are available only to tribal chiefs, and some are considered to be so fearsome that even mentioning their names will cause women and children to flee for fear of dying on the spot.

While the fear-inducing effects of the masks are obvious, their real power lies in how they demonstrate and manage honor within the Salampasu people.

Masks aren't given out freely and each boy or man has to prove himself worthy (useful enough to the tribe) to be granted ownership of a given mask. This worthiness can come from direct actions like hunting well, killing in battle, or leading other men, or indirect actions like attaining enough wealth and resources to afford access to different masks.

The men with the most masks are granted more privileges, have the highest status, and are treated with the highest honor in the group. Whereas those who possess only the basic masks are not seen to be as honorable or as useful to the tribe.

Amongst the Salampasu people, the demonstration of honor is overt. But one thing that can make the communication of honor so interesting is that there is often more nuance than what we would expect.

Take the color orange. If you're a hunter, this color is one that is used for your own safety and to subtly signal that you belong to the community. It can be found on gear and particularly on clothing. The proper amount of orange, worn on the correct types of clothing, can be used to signal status and belonging within the group, in addition to serving the primary purpose of keeping the wearer safe. It is a color that signals a simple form of honor and belonging within that particular community.

However, that same color, when worn in an entire jumpsuit is a symbol of dishonor and complete rejection from civilized society. It's a prisoner's uniform.

The attention-drawing nature of the color is used for the exact opposite reason. Rather than keeping the wearer safe from the other members of society, it is used to warn the world around him, that the wearer is dangerous and a dishonorable member of the tribe.

Let's take this principle and apply it even to our daily lives. It's safe to assume that, whatever you do for a living, the people within your industry all dress fairly similarly. Sure there may be some subtle variations, but even those distinctions contribute to the importance of honor in appearance, rather than detract from it.

Honor is why you don't see many construction workers in suits, attorneys in pajamas, or bankers in flip-flops.

Honor is why most of the Baby Boomer generation dress similarly.

Honor is why your colleagues start to resent you when you improve your appearance.

Most men, especially those who aren't particularly high-status in any given group, will dress to fit in. We will dress to not rock the boat. And we will dress to feel comfortable.

Because to do otherwise is the sin of hubris. We fear it communicates to our peers that we believe we're better than they are and deserve to be seen and treated as such.

And this is because that's what we've been taught a man's proper and honorable relationship with his clothing should be.

The reason caring for your style is seen as effeminate and bad is because it's perceived as dishonorable. It is going against the culturally agreed-upon code of a man's proper relationship with his appearance since the 1960's.

But a pirate, jaguar warrior, or Salampasu man deciding his appearance doesn't matter is an act of betrayal and dishonor within his own culture and expectations.

Thankfully, cultures shift and expectations change and we are seeing the status quo of the only honorable relationship with style being ambivalence starting to crumble around us.

Whenever the point in history, whatever the culture, a man's clothing, grooming, and appearance may not matter much when it comes to acquiring and developing these various masculine virtues, but they are infinitely useful in the internalization and projection of them.

5 CLOTHING IS COMMUNICATION

Have you ever taken the time to think about how incredible a written and spoken language is?

There's a story of an explorer in a remote part of the world who wanted to send a message to a friend a long distance away. He arranged to have a local whom he trusted be his messenger and carry the necessary communication.

The local watched as the explorer used a pen to make some marks on a paper - marks which had no meaning or significance to him. Then the explorer gave the local the paper to be delivered.

After crossing the many miles between the explorer and his friend, the local handed the message to the man for whom it was intended. To his surprise, the local soon learned that, upon examining the pen marks on the paper, the recipient knew exactly where the explorer was and what his problems were. He knew about his health, circumstances, and needs just as well as if he and the explorer had spoken face-to-face.

The miracle of this method of communication was so profound to the local that he knelt down and worshipped the paper.

To us, the ability to read and write is commonplace and taken for granted. But for those who don't understand the function of the written word, it is both a miracle and a mystery.

Most of our communication is socially constructed. The local and the explorer had very different relationships with the markings on the paper. For the explorer, those markings created letters, formed words, and communicated a message. For the local, they were random strokes of a pen that likely had no rhyme, reason, or aesthetic value - let alone any deeper meaning.

The difference between the two men was not an innate ability to understand how to read or write - it was that one was taught how to do so while the other was not.

The modern world will tell you that somehow being a social construct makes something less valuable - as if we need to only embrace what our biology limits us to and everything else is up for grabs.

But you won't attain much success in life if you speak entirely in your own language or never learn to read or write. Everything you're getting from this book comes from the mutual understanding that particular shapes of ink form letters, the organized combinations of those letters create words, and relationships between those words leads to coherent thoughts and understanding between us.

To make things even more difficult, language is not something mutually agreed upon by all people. There are differences in languages, dialects, accents, speech patterns, and even unique biases for or against particular words.

Language is the balance between the group and the individual. By having an agreed-upon standard of what symbols or sounds have meaning, we are able to create communication that can be as individual and nuanced as we intend it to be.

Imagine the monumental task of having to invent a new language every time you wanted to communicate a thought you'd never shared before.

It would be impossible!

However, by "conforming" to the use of particular words - and their meanings - you are able to put them together into complete thoughts and share your communication with those around you.

Clothing is communication. Appearance is language. What we project visually is just as important as what we say audibly.

As we discussed previously, most men only want to dress only so far as to not be embarrassed. They believe that, somehow, choosing to become fluent in the language of aesthetics runs counter to their ability to succeed in the world.

Can you imagine if you had that attitude about your speech? If your concern was speaking just passably well enough to convey content?

"Me hungry."

"Want make money for family"

"Man no care for clothes"

Sure you can understand the meaning of those phrases and could arguably survive without speaking much better than that - but it certainly would limit your ability to succeed.

Thankfully, moving away from this approach doesn't require you to become fluent in nine different languages, have a vocabulary that rivals the dictionary, or join the ranks of the grammar nazis. Wanting to avoid the bare minimum does not automatically mean you're headed toward extremism.

In fact, moving too far in the other direction can often be just as detrimental as keeping language too basic.

But if we can understand the value of being able to speak fluently, comprehend, read, and write a spoken language, why is it so difficult to embrace the same concept with our appearance?

Over the next group of chapters, we'll look at aesthetic communication in the same patterns we see in spoken language.

6 TACTICS VS STRATEGIES

Before diving into this book's approach to style and appearance, I need to explain one more crucial element.

The vast majority of style advice available today is almost 100% tactical. It doesn't matter if you're reading style bibles like Alan Flusser's *Dressing the Man*, watching the biggest names on YouTube, or frequenting the most highly trafficked forums. The one thing each of these has in common is that they teach an overly simplistic approach to execution.

And I don't blame any of them for taking this route. They know what their audience wants, and the vast majority of men would much rather be told "the one shirt they should have in their closet" than be taught how to know which shirt is perfectly suited to help them accomplish a particular goal in their life.

Whether it's in style, business, or the battlefield, tactics are crucial and important, but if they're the only thing you focus on, they become a distraction and can often lead to failure rather than success.

You may be asking yourself what I want you to pay attention to if it's not tactics. Well let me lay it out for you.

In the hierarchy of accomplishment, the first thing you should strive for is a goal. This is a broad, general outcome you're seeking.

Secondary to the goal is the strategy - the approach you take to achieve said goal.

As part of your strategy, you establish objectives - measurable milestones which contribute to the strategy.

And finally, we get back down to tactics, which are the tools you use to accomplish objectives.

To better illustrate this point, let's put it into some context.

Let's say you have a goal of being in better shape. What is your strategy? For most men it involves losing fat, adding muscle, increasing endurance, and recovering from injury more quickly.

The objectives to determine if you're progressing within these various strategies can consist of things like dropping body fat from 20% to 10%, adding 10 pounds of muscle, running five miles comfortably instead of three, or being able to touch your toes.

Note that none of these objectives is valuable in and of itself. It's only because it contributes to the goal of being in better shape (which in reality can be an objective of a broader goal such as living longer, being more attractive, etc.) that there is any worth in being able to touch your toes.

And how are these objectives met? By implementing tactics like counting calories, lifting progressively heavier weights, doing consistent cardio, or stretching daily.

Again, each of these tactics - just like the objectives they help reach - are only worthwhile because of their contribution to the greater goal.

If you had no idea why you were supposed to lift weights consistently and no understanding how it was going to improve your life in multiple ways, how much more difficult would it be to find motivation to go to the gym each morning?

Even if your focus wasn't limited to tactics but capped out at the objectives, how much harder would it be to consistently execute or even care? Without a true understanding of how a low body fat and higher endurance rate can lead to being in better shape and living a better life, it would be easy to ridicule and write off those who invest the time and energy into doing so. In fact, there are plenty of people in the world who do just that - either because they don't understand or don't believe that being in better shape will make them happier and more successful, or because they've convinced themselves they don't need to try.

Thankfully those dots are easy to connect in fitness. They get a little muddier in politics, business, and even strategy games like chess, but they're barely understood when it comes to a man's appearance and style.

From one perspective this makes sense. Like we talked about in the difference between visual power and visual appeal, men and women largely have different goals we're trying to achieve by dressing better.

However, when we don't see the difference between those goals and only focus on the objectives or tactics - it's all too easy to believe that dressing well, caring about style, or putting more than the basic effort into grooming and appearance is effeminate.

Women know their goals. It's first and foremost to compete with other women in the social hierarchy (any woman who says otherwise is lying - either to you or herself, but she's lying) and secondly to be attractive to a man.

Most men don't know their goals. They have a vague understanding that dressing better helps them avoid embarrassment but that's it.

At some point a man will experience a defining moment in his aesthetic life when he's forced to come to terms with his appearance. It may be after seeing photos of himself on vacation, experiencing a rough divorce, not being able to make friends in school, or some other pressure point. Whatever it is, whether it happens when he's 7 or 70, each man will have a moment when he feels and truly understands that a better appearance will be an asset.

Those who experience this young enough or are willing to act on that moment will seek out help in dressing better.

And this is where they will run into the same problem almost all style-conscious men in the 21st century do - they'll find generic, tactic-based advice that assumes all men are after the same objectives and goals.

But from a logical perspective, a 50-year-old man who's just become a C-level executive has very different aesthetic objectives than a college student trying to find a girlfriend.

If you wouldn't expect a farmer who sells milk to follow the exact same business advice as an attorney who's trying to fine-tune his marketing strategy, why would you believe they need the same style advice?

Whether your direction comes from an online influencer, a coach, or yourself, if you don't take the time to think about your goals and objectives for your appearance you're wasting your time getting overly focused on tactics.

If you're trying to become better friends with the men who work on your oil rig, you don't show up to the pub in a bright green sport coat. If you're building a brand centered around the latest smartphone app you've developed you don't walk into meetings with venture capitalists wearing a bathing suit and flip-flops. If you're supporting your son while he's being tried in court, you don't arrive in a baseball cap and a T-shirt.

As you've been on your own journey of sartorial improvement you may have started to adopt some of the tactic-minded approach. For example, if you believe a suit is the only way to dress well, you're focusing too much on tactics.

If you believe that the only place where flip-flops are appropriate is the beach or near a body of water, you're beholden to tactics.

If you've found yourself saying there is never a situation where cargo shorts are appropriate, you're bound by tactics.

Now, before you feel too guilty, defensive, or discouraged, let me give you more context here.

Focusing on tactics is a wonderfully effective approach to learning how to improve your style. After all, even top military generals went through basic training to learn how to fire and clean a weapon.

There is more than enough room for a tactical approach and it's one that should be adopted. In fact, I even lay out some tactics later in this book.

That said, if you stop at tactics, rather than diving in deeper and trying to understand your own objectives, strategies, and goals, your appearance will never communicate any real power. It will always look inauthentic and inconsistent with who you are.

Thankfully, many of the goals, strategies, and objectives you pursue are not entirely unique or individual.

Remember in the last chapter when we were talking about how frustrating it would be if you couldn't speak the language of those around you? Well getting rid of your "umms" and "uhhs" is a tactic. Whereas fluently speaking a language is an objective or even a goal. You don't have to come up with all the answers on your own. In fact, having that attitude or approach will most likely come at your detriment.

The next six chapters outline the primary, universal strategies that are necessary in accomplishing the goal of being well-dressed. Each strategy will have its own objectives and each objective will be laced with its own tactics. While the strategies may be broad and applicable to every man, your own objectives and tactics will be unique.

The purpose of these six chapters is to lay out said strategies and teach you how to properly identify, establish, and execute your objectives and tactics within each of them.

I'm not going to tell you the three essential shoes you need in your closet. Nor am I going to tell you what timeless style looks like. What I am going to do is walk you through necessary principles so you will never have to question what you're wearing ever again.

Once you know these strategies by heart you'll be able to take yourself through the entire process and not spend your time searching for things like, "what to wear to a baby shower" or "which tie knot is best."

7 BODY

The first thing a soldier needs is proper equipment - his boots, weapon, body armor, and other gear. Once he has these tools, he can apply them effectively in any situation. The tools don't make the soldier, they don't make him effective, they don't define the enemy or the objectives, they simply allow him to do the job.

The same principle applies to understanding the "science" of style. There are guidelines to dressing well that involve things like your face shape, skin tone, and body type, and understanding them is a necessary aspect of dressing well and accomplishing your aesthetic goals.

Before we go any deeper into this subject I want to iterate its importance, while still helping you understand it's only one of six key factors. The vast majority of aesthetic coaching, teaching, and training focuses nearly 100% on understanding the science of style.

All the best soldiers are sufficient marksmen, but not all marksmen are the best soldiers. Becoming a master in this field requires mindset, physical strength and endurance, discipline, tenacity, a willingness to embrace risk, and other factors beyond a simple understanding of and capability with weapons and other tools of war.

The best dressed men all know how to dress to their body and its limitations, but not every man who understands the style rules regarding his body is well-dressed. Thankfully, becoming proficient in this field requires infinitely less than what is needed to be an effective soldier. But style comes from more than just knowing what looks good on you. It requires a mindset, discipline, a willingness to embrace risk, and other factors outlined further in this book.

There's one more little caveat to add before jumping into the meat of this chapter. There are a lot of terms, some math, and a ton of potential for confusion when learning about maximizing the visual effects of your body.

Unlike the other elements of style - which are largely conceptual and designed to change your way of thinking, this chapter on body is almost entirely focused on a tactical approach.

Unless you're a super genius or someone with a photographic memory, don't expect to get through this chapter once and fully retain all the information. Plan to reference and re-reference the chapter a few times until you feel you have your own body's strengths and weaknesses determined and accounted for.

That said, let's discuss some of the fundamental principles of knowing your body and dressing well.

Contrast

Your contrast type is determined by the relationship between the color of your hair and the color of your skin. By properly accounting for your contrast type, you are able to ensure that the visual focal point is your face. Proper contrast also makes your countenance appear stronger and more healthy.

This entire concept is laid out masterfully in Alan Flusser's *Dressing the Man* and, for the sake of brevity, will simply be summarized here.

If you have light hair and light skin you have a muted contrast.

If you have dark hair and light skin you have a high contrast.

If you have dark hair and very dark skin you will operate between a medium and high contrast

If you have any variation of skin and hair beyond these three you have a medium contrast.

Now that you know the different contrast type, you need to know why they even matter.

They serve two purposes. The first is to ensure that proper attention is given to your face and not to the clothing around you. If your clothing does not correctly contrast with your given type, it will often distract from, rather than contribute to any attention being paid to you.

The second reason is because it works to help your skin look healthy and vibrant. If you're a high-contrast man, then your natural vitality is best complemented through high-contrast clothing - otherwise you can look dampened or drab.

The same applies regardless of your contrast type. By not using color variation in a way that complements it, you end up looking less healthy and happy than you could otherwise.

I'm sure you remember learning about the color wheel in grade school. Well the relationship each color has with each other, on that wheel, can either help or hurt your appearance.

To better understand how this all works with each contrast type, here are a few key terms.

The easiest example of this is with the basic, six-color color wheel. However, as different, more subtle shades and hues are added in, the principles still apply, albeit with a bit more leniency to the exact relationship each color has with its corresponding shades. To see visual examples of this, visit www.appearanceofpower.com/colors

Essentially, this can be as simple or as complicated as you'd like to make it.

Here are the three primary terms for our purposes.

Contrasting - colors that lie opposite each other on the color wheel - red/green, blue/orange, yellow/purple, etc.

Triadic - colors that can be separated by equal thirds on the color wheel - orange/green/purple or red/yellow/blue.

Analogous - colors that lie next to each other on the color wheel - red/purple/blue, orange/yellow/green, yellow/green/blue, etc.

The relationships these colors have with each other matter, because of the way their light frequency affects a viewers eye. When two colors are opposite each other on the wheel, seeing them together is jarring and noticeable. The opposite effect is achieved when colors that are similar to each other are all placed together.

By understanding the relationship each color has to its counterparts, and then knowing what combinations work best with your own contrast type, you become capable of dressing in a way that keeps you looking healthy, energetic, and powerful.

Most people won't be able to quantify why you look good, but they'll be able to notice a difference.

Now that we've established the basics of the color wheel and the importance of using contrast to keep you looking your best, let's go over how each contrast type works best within the color wheel.

If you have a medium contrast you have the blessing and the curse of being able to wear nearly any color combination you like - whether the colors be triad, contrasting, or analogous - as long as they work with your skin tone (more on that later). The key is to experiment and find what best suits your individual taste and needs - all of which can be determined by factoring in the other elements of style.

If you have a high contrast you need a stronger variation on color. Your primary focus should be on contrasting colors, with a secondary focus on triad colors. For the most part, analogous colors should be avoided.

If you have a muted contrast your face will be overwhelmed by too much variation in color. Therefore your primary focus should be analogous, with a secondary focus on triad colors. For the most part, contrasting color should be avoided.

One thing to understand about contrast is it's not nearly as important in an overall outfit as it is with different accessories that are near your face.

For example, if you have a high contrast and decide to wear a pair of blue jeans, this does not mean your only shirt options are either white or orange. You can wear a different shade of blue and have it work just fine. Because the contrast point between the pants and shirt is so far away from your face, you don't need to be overly worried with their visual effects - simply make sure the colors work well together.

However, if you have a high contrast and are wearing a suit and tie - a navy suit, with blue shirt, purple tie, and purple pocket square won't work very well. Those colors are all too similar to each other and close to your face. By introducing some contrast in your shirt, accessories, or both, you'll frame your face much better.

Just like any other tactic you'll learn, use color theory when it's appropriate. If you're attending an all-white event and expected to wear one color, don't sweat not having any contrast to your face. The other goals and objectives of said event will override the need for this particular tactic.

To bring it back into the strategy vs tactics approach, we can look at it this way:

Goal: Draw attention to face not clothes and make face look healthy and vibrant

Strategy: Employ color strategy that works with contrast type

Tactics: Wear black suit, white shirt, purple tie, and gold pocket square to create the strongest contrast possible.

Face Shape

Over the years there have been a multitude of studies conducted which show that facial symmetry - the even placement of facial features - is strongly correlated with attraction. Those with more facial symmetry are seen as more attractive, more trustworthy, and more likable than those who have an imbalance - however slight those imbalances may be.

Similar studies have also concluded that attractiveness can be measured across differing individuals and cultures, implying that a more objective standard of beauty exists and can be capitalized on.

This observation isn't new either. The ancient Greeks believed in a system of physiognomy which is founded on the idea that the character and body of a man are interconnected, that our bodies - and particularly our faces change - as we develop certain character traits, and that we can determine the strength of a person's character by looking at his face.

Physiognomy has seen popularity throughout different stages of history but is currently perceived as a pseudo science. However, even those who disagree with the veracity of determining a man's character from his face have acknowledged that people regularly make judgments based on clothing, facial features, and other visual indicators, that these same judgments are shared by other people, and that these judgments even occur cross culturally.

Which all basically means that we act as if physiognomy is real and relevant, regardless of whether or not it actually is.

While you cannot control if someone is going to judge you by how you look or whether or not those evaluations will be accurate, you can affect and control for the factors used to make the assessment.

So, what does the ideal man's face shape look like?

Well, it's time for a little math. Not too much, but just a bit.

Both the ideal face shape and optimal body proportions (more on that a little later) can be measured by using "phi" ($\Phi = 1.618033988749895...$), also known as the golden ratio.

Phi was used by ancient Greeks and during the Renaissance by sculptors, painters, architects, and myriad other builders and designers. It also exists in nature and is the basis by which we measure proportional beauty and attractiveness.

It is a ratio determined by the relationship between different line segments and how they are divided by each other.

For example, let's suppose we have three lines: A,B, and C

Line A is the total length of line B added to line C.

The difference in length between lines A and B, is the same proportionate distance in length between lines B and C.

So if line A is 5.24 feet long, line B is 3.24 feet long, and line C is 2.0 feet long, we have the golden ratio. By dividing line C by phi (1.618...) we get line B and by multiplying line B by phi we get line A.

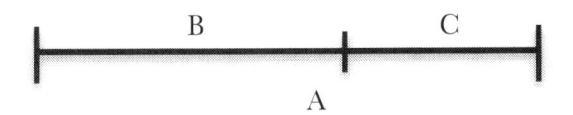

Ok, that's it for the math.

You may be asking yourself what this all has to do with face shape.

The golden ratio can be applied across the human face in a multitude of ways - the distance from the eyes to the flare of the nostrils to the base of the nose, eyes to nostril top to lip center, side of face to outside of eyes to center of eyes, side of face to center of face to outside of opposite eye, and plenty of others.

Now, it's both unreasonable and a little excessive to expect you to figure out which parts of your face go beyond the golden ratio and then apply custom made collars, glasses, hats, and haircuts that will provide the ideal visual balance to make your face look as close to the golden ratio as possible.

To make it all more feasible and easier to create a visual golden ratio, we'll use a system that has been in place for thousands of years - grouping faces by their shape.

Since ancient Greece, the ideal shape has been an oval. It implies perfect symmetry and balance - the ideal for beauty in both men and women. A perfectly oval face consists of two characteristics:

1 - The length of the face is 1.618 times its width. This is indicative of a healthy level of fat in the body. Faces that are wider than this ratio can appear too fat, soft, or even childlike. Faces that are narrower will appear gaunt, unhealthy, or unnatural.

2 - The width of the forehead is the same width as the jaw. Both a strong jaw and a strong brow are correlated to higher levels of testosterone, making these visual indicators of strength, dominance, health, virility, and other masculine traits.

Unfortunately not all of us have the advantage of perfectly (or near perfectly) symmetrical faces. It's easy to think this means we're relegated to mix with other "ugly" people and let the more attractive gain all the positive attention.

However, there are stylistic and aesthetic measures that can be taken which will help to provide better facial balance and symmetry than what you may have been born with.

By playing around with collar types, the shape of glasses and sunglasses, tie knots, beard shapes, and hair cuts, you can provide "balance" to your face and project more visual symmetry than what you otherwise have.

The further your face shape varies from an oval, the more limited your choices and the more important balance is.

For example, round faces need long collars and deep, aviator style glasses. Both of these visually lengthen the face to help compensate for its roundness and visually get it closer to the neutral oval.

The opposite is the case for long faces which need wide, spread collars and wider glasses to provide the same essential balance and help the face appear more neutral.

Pattern & Proportion

The Golden Ratio doesn't merely work with your face shape; it's equally applicable to the overall proportions of your entire body.

For example the length of your shin should be 1.618 times the length of your foot; the length of your forearm should be 1.618 times the length of your hand; your total height should be 1.618 times the length of your legs, which should be 1.618 times the length of your arms, etc.

As much as you can influence your facial symmetry through variables like collars and glasses, you can control for your body's proportions even more. This is where understanding your body and what prevents it from appearing as a perfect Phi can go a long way toward helping you dress better.

Because, as interesting as the physiology of the human body is, what's more applicable to us is the psychology behind all of this. Our brains are wired to seek balance and symmetry wherever they can and not only to search them out but to be attracted to them and create them. When we say someone has an attractive face or a great build, what we're really saying is there's good symmetry - symmetry determined by the Golden Ratio.

Essentially, the more your body complies with the Golden Ratio, the more powerful and attractive you'll look - both physiologically and psychologically. And, while your body is already based off principles of balance and symmetry, and these ratios can be impacted by diet and exercise, it begs the question - how does your clothing affect this and what are the main proportions you should be looking for?

While it is possible to pay attention to variables like the length of the arms and legs in comparison to each other and to your overall height, the most glaringly obvious and important ratio is the relationship between your shoulders and waist.

Remember when we talked about the tactical virtue of strength and how a suit can help most men attain the ideal V shape? Then the idea that broad shoulders are attractive, powerful, and masculine should come as no surprise to you. However, "broad" is a relative term that doesn't have a distinct quantity. Do shoulders that are three times as large as your waist look better than those that are only two? What about only twice as wide or half as wide? Do those effects set each other off at some point?

As you may have guessed, the ideal balance between the waist and the shoulders is 1.618

One of the best ways to help visually create this golden ratio between shoulders and waist is through the use of patterns in your clothing.

Patterns can affect your body's visual symmetry and will do so via three different methods: size, type, and intensity. All three variables can work independently or in conjunction with one another to improve or worsen your aesthetic and each should be considered before making a purchase.

In order to maximize the full effect of pattern, we'll discuss them from two different angles: size and type. Each of these has merit on its own and can be used to minimize or enhance certain visual cues.

While the size of a pattern can affect formality in some cultures, it is a more subjective standard and will not be discussed in depth in this book. A simple guide to follow, in Western culture, is that the larger the pattern, the more casual the garment.

Much more crucial than its relationship to formality, is the effect a pattern's size will have on your proportions.

As logic would dictate, larger men should wear larger patterns and smaller men should wear smaller patterns. Proportion is a fundamental aspect of dressing well.

Large men appear hulking when wearing patterns that are too small.

Small men appear miniature when wearing patterns that are too large.

In general, if you wear XL T-shirts or larger (and they fit you properly), you should avoid small patterns. If you wear Small T-shirts or smaller you should avoid large patterns. If you wear Large or Medium T-shirts you can work with all pattern sizes.

Different pattern types have different pattern effects and should be utilized accordingly. They are as follows:

Vertical stripes add visual height and elongation, along with making you appear slimmer. So, if you look too broad for your height, wearing this pattern will help visually balance your proportions.

Horizontal stripes add visual weight and visually cut you into distinct segments, making you appear shorter. Meaning, if you're too tall and/or too skinny for your breadth, wearing this pattern will help make you appear wider and closer to the ideal.

Boxes and checks add visual heft, making you appear larger overall. Even if your proportions are ideal, you may just want to look a little bigger than you are.

Both height and weight perceptions are affected by stripe variations and should be considered when purchasing various patterns. Different body types benefit from different patterns.

If your proportions make you look too long and tall for how wide you are, you should be cautious about wearing vertical stripes. This pattern draws the eyes up, which will over accentuate your already narrow proportions. By wearing a stripe that is comparatively wider, this effect can be minimized.

Horizontal stripes, in all gauges and sizes, will flatter you by visually cutting you down into segments. By blocking the natural upward flow of the viewers eyes, more visual weight is added to your overall proportions.

Boxes, checks, and plaids serve a similar function as horizontal stripes, but also maintain a bit of the upward flow of the viewers eyes. These patterns can help you appear more muscular.

If your body type is the opposite - wider in proportion than it should be - you should focus primarily on wearing vertical stripes. You will benefit from the pattern drawing peoples' eyes up and helping create a Phi-like proportion.

The goal is to balance out your broader proportions. The narrower the stripe, the more exaggerated the effect. However, caution should be exercised in not going beyond a stripe size that is inconsistent with your overall stature.

Horizontal stripes, in all gauges and sizes, should be avoided. They will over-accentuate areas of extra weight and will also visually cut you into shorter segments, throwing your proportions even further away from the Golden Ratio.

Boxes, checks, and plaids serve a similar function as vertical stripes, but also maintain a bit of the outward flow of the viewers eyes. These patterns should be worn in proportion and with caution.

If your body is built in or close to the Golden Ratio, you are still free to wear patterns. They can look interesting and add some visual variety and aesthetic balance, even if you don't need them to help your overall proportions.

Keep in mind that the same visual effects are created, vertical stripes will narrow you out, horizontal stripes will broaden you, and boxes and checks will add more heft. As long as you embrace these aspects, you'll be fine to wear whatever pattern you prefer.

By knowing both the proportion and type of patterns you should embrace and avoid, you'll be better dressed, and better looking than 90% of your peers. You'll look healthier, more successful, and more powerful.

Skin Tone

The final, general aspect of understanding your body is also the most difficult to quantify and master.

Irrespective of your race, origin, or skin color, you have a particular skin tone. It's an area that the women's beauty and cosmetic industry has completely dialed in and there are dozens of different shades of makeup women can choose from to perfectly match their tone, and yet there are still women who are incapable of finding one that perfectly fits their needs.

Thankfully, we're not talking or worrying about makeup. You don't have to perfectly and precisely match a bunch of different products to the exact shade, tone, and cast of your face.

However, by knowing a bit about the difference between two families of color, you will be able to use the process of elimination to make buying new clothes easier and be able to wear colors that always make you look healthy and energetic.

The two most simple color classifications are warm and cool. Warm colors are those that are gold-based and tend to reflect the colors you see in nature during spring and autumn. Cool colors are blue-based and reflect the colors you see in nature during summer and winter.

This does not mean that you can only wear blue if you have cool skin or yellow if you have warm skin. There are plenty of shades of warm blues and cool yellows.

To see a visual guide on the differences between these two families and examples of a range of both warm and cool colors, head on over to www.appearanceofpower.com/colors.

There are a few methods to determining what your skin tone is. The first is to take a look at the veins on the inside of your forearm. If they look more blue, it's likely your tone is cool. If they appear green (or greenish), you're warm.

Think of the mixing of colors. Blue and blue still make a blue. Whereas blue and yellow make green.

The second method is to try on some neutrals. Head into a suit shop - they'll typically have a broader selection of colors to work with then a more casual clothing store - and ask to try on a few different suits.

Experiment with different cloths in black, charcoal, and light grey. Then a few in ivory, brown, and olive. You can do the same thing with a stark white shirt and and off-white shirt if you prefer.

Remember not to focus on the difference in formality, cut, or design of the different suits or their colors. The purpose of this particular exercise isn't to buy the right garments, it's to figure out if you look better in cool (black, white, grey) or warm (ivory, brown, off-white) tones.

Focus on your face and your skin. Does one group make you look tired and ashen? Does the other make you appear healthier and more energetic?

It may be difficult to tell this about yourself and, unless you're in a shop with a highly-trained staff, they probably won't be able to help you out either. So, this is the one time I'd strongly recommend bringing a wife, girlfriend, daughter, or some other female friend along. She's not there to help you choose a suit, which means she won't sway you toward her aesthetic goals over yours. She's there because she's been indoctrinated with the importance of skin tones even as a pre-teen and has a more developed eye for the concept.

Be patient with this part of the process as it can be extremely subtle and difficult to assess initially. If you don't feel like you can get a good grasp on it right away, there are some default colors that are worth sticking with. These are white, grey, brown, blue, black, and burgundy.

Regardless of your skin tone, you'll be able to work with these different colors and create something flattering. When you're ready to start moving beyond, into shades of green, yellow, purple, and orange, is when you'll want to be sure you know your skin tone and what's most flattering on you.

At this point you may be asking yourself about fit. After all, fit is king, or so the mantra of almost every style guru goes and a proper fit can override every single other aspect of dressing to your body.

Unfortunately a proper fit is not an objective measure. Take a look at the suit - a garment that has fundamentally changed very little over the past century. However, within that time period we've seen full, boxy cuts in the 1940's, narrower silhouettes with small lapels in the 60's, massive shoulders and overly baggy shapes in the 90's, and the hyper-skinny fits of the 2010's.

It's tempting to say that moderation is key and a timeless garment - be it a suit or some other piece of clothing - is one that equally avoids being too baggy or too skinny. While this may be true to some extent, avoiding particular swings in fashion and style comes with its own costs - which brings us back to the understanding that one particular tactic isn't always going to be the best to pursue.

Yes you can invest in a quality suit with a middle-of-the-road fit. But there are tribal and cultural signals that you're either sending or failing to send by not conforming to or rebelling against the dominant fit of the time.

Moderation may be the perfect tactic for you, but that doesn't make it the ideal approach for every man. Once again, the potential risks and rewards of adopting a particular fit need to be addressed before making a purchase.

Ultimately this same measure applies to all standards of the body. Yes we're biologically wired to seek for symmetry and balance, but maybe your goals are better accomplished with dissonance. As a result, you should intentionally skew away from Phi and over-exaggerate one proportion over another.

Maybe you have a Stark contrast but want attention drawn away from your face. In this case you should be wearing similar colors and avoiding those that are opposite each other on the wheel.

Or, perhaps you're not feeling great and need to help sell that fact even more - so, although you have a cool complexion, you put on warm colors in order to subtly give off an appearance that's a bit more sickly and off balance.

Your approach to how you use the rules of the body should always conform to what your goals are and not the other way around.

Once you have a basic understanding of your body and how appearance is affected by biology and mathematics, it's time to move on to the next component - Archetype.

8 ARCHETYPE

Now that you know the importance of your body, its strengths and limitations, and how to use clothing within that understanding, dressing well is going to be incredibly easy, right?

Well not quite. Because, even though there are objective, scientific rules about what is and is not pleasing to the eye, those rules make up a minority of what it means to be stylish.

Think of it this way. Deciding you want to dress better is about as nebulous and undefinable as saying you want to get in better shape. And yes, we've used the fitness metaphor already in this book, but there are a lot of correlations and it's worth visiting again.

There may be a few things that are consistent amongst all people who are in good shape - they don't have excess amounts of body fat, they are in charge of their bodies rather than letting their bodies control them, they have a healthy relationship with food, etc. - but there is a whole range of ideal bodies.

Take a look at the different athletes in the Olympics. Swimmers, gymnasts, marathoners, and boxers all have varying physiques. Their bodies look different, they function differently, and they are used to accomplish different goals.

Can you say a boxer or basketball player is in objectively better shape than a running back? Are long-distance runners healthier than sprinters? What about those who start to blur the lines like sumo wrestlers and power lifters? Their bodies don't even aesthetically line up with some of the basic tenets of being in shape, but does that mean those men are unhealthy?

If you were to decide today that you wanted to get in better shape, what would you do?

It's likely you'd start watching what you eat, sleeping better, and decreasing the stress in your life. What about your exercise? Would you start jogging and just focus on that? Would you start playing a sport and have that be your primary form of movement? Would you join a gym and start lifting weights? If so, would you be more inclined to follow the programs you'd find as a powerlifter or a bodybuilder? Maybe even a cross fitter?

There are so many directions you can head, and that's the point. There may be a few simple standards of being in shape, but there is a huge variety of ways that goal can both be attained and manifested.

The same can be applied for your style and appearance.

There may be a few things that are underlying threads amongst all people who dress well - their clothes fit in a way that flatters their body and face, they deliberately choose what they wear rather than letting aesthetic inertia lead the way, they have a healthy relationship with appearance, etc. - but there is a whole range of ideal styles.

Take a look at the different men's aesthetics throughout history. Feudal Japan, ancient Sparta, and Renaissance Italy all had men dressing completely differently. Their overall styles looked different, the materials they used were unique, and their clothing was used to manifest distinct, desirable traits. And, lest you think these variations only exist in different time periods or national cultures, pay attention to how many different styles are seen in the West today.

Can you say a business man in a tailored suit is objectively more stylish than the singer of a popular band? Are ties better than leather jackets? What about those who start to blur the lines like the East Coast preppy who combines the dignity of traditionally British clothing and the rakishness of bold colors and loud patterns? Their appearances don't even aesthetically line up with some of the basic tenets of being well dressed, but does that mean those men are not stylish?

If you were to decide today that you wanted to look better what would you do?

It's likely you'd start by throwing out the clothes that don't fit, getting a better haircut, and buying new items for your closet. But what would you buy? Would you start with a suit and only wear that? Would you buy ten exact pieces consisting of the same shirt and pants and create a personal uniform that never varied? Would you ask your friends, wife, or co-workers how they suggest you look? If so, would you be more inclined to follow the advice you'd get from the people at work, your family, or your childhood friends?

At this point you're probably feeling a bit overwhelmed. What might have seemed like a relatively easy process all of a sudden appears much more complicated and in-depth than you want it to be - hence the reason most men hate thinking about clothing and loathe shopping even more.

Most of us haven't been taught the right way to approach this aspect of our lives, and feel inadequate when it's time to do so. So, in a sour-grapes attitude of, "if I can't do it right I'll convince myself it's unimportant" many of us start to tell ourselves that dressing well doesn't matter. When really, we just need to know how to move in the right direction.

Going back to our fitness analogy - if you were to be asked what you prioritized more between endurance, muscle proportions, and physical strength, would that make it easer for you to determine what it meant for you to be in good shape?

If you enjoy jogging and like the leanness of a long-distance runner's build, it probably doesn't make sense to be focusing on improving your deadlift each week. If you want to get as strong as possible, it won't do you much good to bench press 85 pounds 100 times.

Knowing what being in shape means to you, what you'd like your body to be capable of, and the actions and habits of other people who are in the shape you'd like to be all of a sudden make it easier to mentally establish a goal and start working towards it. That undefinable "be in better shape" now means, I want to be able to lift my own bodyweight over my head, run a sub 6:00 minute mile, and be able to look great in a bathing suit.

Those are definable, visible accomplishments and determine the kind of work you'll be doing to accomplish them.

The same attitude and approach are applicable for your appearance. While wanting to look better can mean a variety of things, it becomes easier to narrow it down once you know your relationship with the world and how your appearance can help facilitate that.

This is where the idea of a style archetype comes in. An archetype is an embodiment of an idea - often a visual representation of an attitude, belief, or approach, something that perfectly represents a standard.

Remember earlier when we talked about the difference between tactics, objectives, strategies, and goals? Well you can think of your archetype as the overarching strategy of the mission. All the objectives and tactics should be considered in light of how they contribute to the overall archetype.

Over the years I've come to find that there are three primary archetypes and they are:

Rugged, Refined, and Rakish.

Just as different olympic sports have unique, distinguishing factors that keep each class grouped together and separate from the others, the three archetypes have distinct definitions.

The Rugged Man is one who is physically masculine. He bends nature to his will by means of his brute force and has a cave-man attitude that tolerates no nonsense. There is nothing subtle about the rugged man and everything in his life exists for a specific, direct purpose. He is the adventurer, the mountain man, the gladiator, and the blue-collar worker.

Rugged men fit very comfortably into traditional, physical definitions of masculinity. Their power and influence often comes from their physical stature, ability and willingness to engage in violence, skill with and affinity for physical tools, and a desire to engage with the natural world.

Many Rugged men prefer the simplicity of nature to the complication of society and value strength and courage - both moral and physical - over other virtues.

Which is not to say that, in order to fall into this archetype that you need to embody each and every one of these traits. But there does need to be an affinity for the physical world.

The Refined Man is one who is financially and influentially masculine. He bends the world of men to his will by means of his connections, his money, and his political and/or social power. He is capable of mixing both direct and subtle elements to accomplish his ends and has so much clout that he very rarely has to adapt to situations going out of his control (because they never do). He is the titan of industry, the politician, the hedge fund manager, and the 1%.

Refined men are often experts in understanding social hierarchies. They enjoy structure and rules and often find their success through accurately navigating a man-made world.

They embody the virtue of honor - even if only in appearance - and are able to use the innate desire for order and structure to attain success - by organizing both their own lives and the lives of those over whom they have influence.

Many Refined men lack a physical power or presence but make up for it through their social and financial capital. Their power is more indirect than direct but that doesn't make it any less effective. They value civilization, with all of its limitations and freedoms, over the chaos of anarchy or tribalism.

You don't have to be at the top of the social hierarchy to be a Refined man. You do, however, need to be a man who respects and adheres to structure, tends to think and behave more rationally than emotionally, and honor both tradition and the importance that other people play in your life.

The Rake is a man who is socially masculine. He influences individual people to his will by means of his attitude, his charisma, and his disdain for following the rules of society and being beholden to another man. While he is capable of using direct elements to accomplish his goals, he lives largely in a subtle world and is always thinking two or three steps ahead of the people around him. He is constantly adapting to new situations and thrives in his ability to do so. He is the playboy, the rock star, the outlaw, and the vigilante.

The term "Rake" has an interesting origin. It stems from the British Royal Navy during the colonial era.

During that time, an important aspect of the maintenance of a ship was truing its mast - that is keeping it straight and upright. Ships that didn't meet the standard of rising perpendicular to the deck were "raked" or "rakish" and their slant was easily recognized from a distance.

The one group the British Royal Navy believed was incapable and/or unwilling to maintain a straight standard for their ships (and their lives) was pirates.

Eventually the term became a slang name for these buccaneers and came to be associated with haughtiness and a disdain for social normalcy or polite society.

Not only were pirates' ships raked, so was everything else about their relationship with Western civilization.

Like the Refined man, the Rake is one who is more comfortable in the world of man than of nature. However, unlike his Refined counterpart, the Rake gets ahead not through adherence to tradition and respect for the rules, but by his willingness to go against them.

Most Rakes are creative types - artists, musicians, photographers, etc. But not all creative types are Rakes. Creativity itself does not equate to social rebellion and you would be wise to not create too simplistic of a link between the two.

Rakes also may be loners but don't have to be. Going back to the origin of the word and the group of men it represented - pirates didn't live in utter anarchy. There were expectations and honor both within individual crews and amongst pirates in general.

Of course these codes didn't have the same weight or bearing as laws, but they did help maintain some level of cohesion and cooperation amongst the various crews.

Rakes are more loyal to themselves or their own specific subcultures and tribes than they are to society in general. They are happy to follow the rules when it serves their, or their gang's purposes, but once they come at odds with the rest of the world, they're always loyal to themselves and their own.

The power in rakishness doesn't stem from physical strength like the Rugged man, nor from financial and social gravitas like the Refined man - rather from a willingness to engage in social risk and the ability to make those risks work to the Rake's advantage.

In summation:

- Rugged - primarily interacts with the world physically - comfortable in nature and enjoys working with his hands.

- Refined - primarily interacts with the world socially, particularly through finances and social status - loves rules, hierarchy, and tradition.

- Rakish - primarily interacts with the world socially, particularly through rebellion and standing out - loves social risk, breaking rules, and standing out from the crowd.

Now that you know the three archetypes, this next piece of information is crucial. They are not mutually exclusive. There is room for variation within the three and it's highly likely you'll have a strong blend of two or even all three of them. You may be primarily within the Rugged, but that doesn't mean you won't have elements that are Refined or Rakish.

Take Teddy Roosevelt as an example. The man was the epitome of the Rugged archetype. He was physically tough and imposing, even completing a speech after he'd been shot in an assassination attempt.

At the same time, he was a Refined man who knew how to dress in a way that met his station as president of the United States. He did not attend meetings or address the nation in his work clothes but did so in well-fitting suits that conformed to the styles of the time.

Roosevelt understood that both his ruggedness and refinement were core components of who he was as a man (even if he didn't think in terms of archetypes like I've presented here). In fact, men like Roosevelt believed the only way to truly be a man was to combine the strengths of these archetypes and minimize their weaknesses.

When we look back to Donovan's four tactical virtues of masculinity, they all can be embodied in each of the three archetypes, albeit in very different forms.

It's easy to see how strength and courage are manifested in the Rugged archetype. After all, these are men who engage with the world in a way that requires both. Mastery can be demonstrated through traditional Rugged activities like tracking game, crafting weapons, and navigating unknown territories.

But even today's manifestations of the Rugged man demonstrate levels of mastery. From auto-mechanics, to rodeo hands, to rock climbers, to weapons specialists, men who are truly capable of altering nature to fit their purposes all attain some form of mastery.

Honor is also apparent in many forms of the Rugged archetype - through things like a respect for nature and her power, a willingness to fight and die for men and women they've never met, adherence to lines drawn and rules established, and an understanding that very few men truly want to live alone.

Refined men may easily demonstrate mastery - social, financial, intellectual, philosophical - and honor. But they also can represent different variations of courage and strength.

It may not take physical courage to run for and attain public office, rise above your peers and climb to a higher position within an organization, or reject a world that's descending into nihilism and mediocrity, but it certainly takes social courage.

And it may not require physical strength to raise a family into productive members of the tribe, manage an organization of thousands of men and women whose lives depend on you, or work 16-hour days in order to realize your aspirations, but it does require mental and emotional strength to do so.

Rakes may easily show their courage and their mastery in their willingness to be or become social outcasts and their ability to take that rejection and use it to their advantage. But that does not mean they are without strength or honor.

Just as we talked about with early pirates, many Rakes only fit the description because they are more loyal to a subculture than to all of humanity - which does not mean they are incapable of honor or loyalty. It simply is manifested in smaller doses and increments than by those who see everyone as their brother or sister.

And the emotional and mental strength required to truly go against the grain and learn to thrive while being on the skirts of, or as a complete outcast to, society are not to be underestimated.

Once you understand your primary archetype, you have a direction in which you can begin to head. And from there, you can pepper in aesthetic elements from the other archetypes to reflect how you personally identify with all three. If you're a Rake, it will do you very little good to dress in a way that's primarily Rugged or Refined, as the elements of these aesthetics can run counter to your goals.

However, if you're a Rake who also has Refined components, then completely rejecting the styles of the Refined archetype can also be limiting.

Once again, let's take a look at this from an objective and strategic standpoint.

If you are a mix between Rugged and Rakish, it means that your primary interactions with the world are based on your physical nature and your willingness to stand out.

If physical capacity and rule breaking are two of your objectives, how does your appearance contribute to that overall objective?

Remember to think about this from the perspective of strategies and goals, not just tactics.

A simplistic approach is to think that all Rugged men wear boots, so you need to wear boots in order to properly dress to your Archetype. But that may not be the case for a small percentage of the time or even at all.

The tactic of wearing boots is one way to accomplish the objective of dressing to suit the rugged archetype, but it may not be the best, and it certainly isn't the only one.

As you're seeing now (and this will become even more evident as we dive deeper in) creating your ideal aesthetic won't be easy. It requires a lot of mental energy and forethought. You need to think one, two, or even three steps down the road to understand the consequences of your decisions.

Thankfully, it becomes easier as you get better at it, and requires less objective effort as you make more progress.

You can see why - even if you know everything about your body, face shape, and skin tone, it's not enough to dress appropriately.

Each of those factors can be addressed as well in a suit as they can in some streetwear or tactical apparel.

Remember how I told you that clothing is communication? Well if that's true, then your Archetype is your language. It's the same as what many other people speak and different from what even more do.

There are certain rules that need to be followed in order to properly speak the language and become adept in its use. You may live in a way that requires you to fluently speak multiple languages (dress to different Archetypes) or simply speak a mixed language that combines elements of two or more.

However, as you know, not every person or group who speaks a language does so the same way. For example, English within the United States is very different in the deep south than it is near the Great Lakes, which is unique compared to the Mexican border in Texas and that's unique compared to what's spoken in Boston. And even then, the English spoken in the US is distinct from what's used in South Africa, Australia, or the United Kingdom.

Sure, we can all understand each other, but that doesn't mean we're speaking the same language. And those little variations can either be a barrier or a way to enhance our relationships with other people.

Those dialects are akin to the next component in learning to dress more intentionally - Tribe.

9 TRIBE

In his book *On Killing* Lt. Colonel Dave Grossman devotes a segment to helping his readers understand what can motivate a man to kill another human being or die facing one.

Contrary to popular belief, the primary motivator is not something like religious conviction, hatred of the enemy, or even a sense of self preservation - it's, "a powerful sense of accountability to his comrades on the battlefield."

Think about that for a minute - the strongest driving factor in convincing men to do the unspeakable is concern for other people - both their well being and their opinion of us.

This whole idea runs contrary to the standardized belief that "a real man doesn't care what anyone else thinks of him" and also introduces some nuance that needs to be taken into account.

The average modern American man - rich or poor, white collar or blue, strong or weak, fat or fit, has a false dichotomy in his brain about his relationship with other men.

He either cares too much what everyone else thinks of him, or he tries to convince himself he doesn't care about anyone else's opinion.

As if, somehow those are the only two options and if he's not walking down the first path, he's forced to tread the second.

The latter mindset is the one I have encountered most during my time writing on men's clothing. Typically I don't read or hear it directly leveled at me, but on forums that link to my channel or site.

These conversations are always dominated by one or two men - typically defending their choice of cargo shorts, super hero T-shirts, and combat boots - who will say, "A real man doesn't care what anyone thinks of him" or "A real man dresses however he wants and doesn't care what anyone says."

Rather than factoring in virtues like honor and loyalty - virtues which absolutely depend on reputation and how other men perceive us and interact with us, these keyboard warriors - and other men like them - have convinced themselves that a crucial component of masculinity is thinking only of yourself and taking only your own opinions and estimations seriously.

It's a justifiable misunderstanding. So much of the Western (and especially American) lionization of masculinity comes from the perception that real men are lone wolves.

We grow up looking at cowboys, outlaws, and rebels as the epitome of masculinity. And all too often, these characterizations include the idea that these men weren't accountable to anyone but themselves.

Ironically, the men who claim to dress however they want, all end up looking exactly the same - like they're wearing some sort of tribal uniform that marks their membership within a specific group.

Contrast the man who doesn't care about the opinion of others with the opposite ideology - the global citizen - the man who claims that all people are equal and that he is attempting to love them all equally and the same. He doesn't believe in the concepts of "us" and "them" because in his ideal world, there are no distinctions between different peoples, cultures, groups, or goals.

In the time it's taken you to read from the beginning of this chapter multiple people have died, killed, been abused, lost a loved one, suffered a debilitating injury, and/or experienced any number of tragedies and victories.

Do you feel anything for those people?

Does the death of a child on the other side of the world impact you the same as if it were your own son? Should it?

In the 1990's, anthropologist Robin Dunbar proposed a theory that the maximum number of people the human mind is capable of maintaining stable social relationships with is 150.

Most of you probably have more friends than that on Facebook.

So let's take those Facebook friends as a smaller example. Would you say you care about each of them equally - that reading about a promotion from your brother is the same as when it happens to a guy you haven't spoken with since high school?

How many of those friends are people you could depend on if you were to lose your job or have car trouble on the side of the road?

How many lead lives worthy of your respect and appreciation, rather than just existing or getting by?

If you had to prioritize them into groups of "would spend a weekend with," "could spend a weekend with," and "would not spend a weekend with," how difficult would it really be to rank and prioritize which person would fall into which group?

How about if someone in another country recommended a movie, song, or piece of clothing? Would that recommendation have the same influence on you as it would coming from a friend or family member?

Now take all of those questions and apply them to people whom you've never met but who live in your city, then your region, then your country.

It quickly becomes easy to see that we're incapable of seeing and treating everyone as equals - that it's impossible to mourn the death of a stranger the same as a loved one - that your day-to-day life is only impacted by success or tragedy when it involves someone whom you truly love, admire, and are loyal to.

Whether we like it or not, humans are tribal. Even if we're capable of seeing each individual as objectively equal in value - we can't and don't give them equal worth from our own subjective relationships and perspectives.

So if we're still supposed to care what people think of us, but we're also incapable of caring about everyone equally, what's the solution?

The answer is fairly easy, but it gets glossed over or passed by all too often - we're supposed to care what the right people think of us.

This is another mindset shift and one that can often be very difficult to make, especially because it runs so counter to a global culture in which we are constantly being bombarded with anti-tribal messaging.

One method I've personally implemented to get my mind right on this concept is a basic one - a person has to earn the right for his opinion to matter to me.

Consider how simple that is. It's easy to give that power away, to let a random commenter on the Internet, a stranger at the airport, or an acquaintance you haven't spoken with for years have an impact on your life.

If a person doesn't have the full context of who you are and what you're trying to accomplish, if he doesn't have any loyalty to you and your well-being, if he hasn't proven that he's vested in your best interest -

why in the world would you let his opinion of you have any sway over your actions?

Any man or woman should earn the right for their opinion of you to matter, and those who have, well their opinion should carry a great deal of weight.

The reality is, people are tribal. We want to spend time with those who act, look, think, and believe like we do.

Tribalism can exist on any scale. History has shown the rise and fall of nations and empires, the quick creation and dissemination of religious ideologies and identities, economic classes of people who cling to their own and discourage others from attempting to break rank, and units as small as two-person couples who share the same last name and become a family.

Tribal separation, like many of the concepts discussed in this book, is an amoral construct. Some tribes' sole purpose is the eradication of the other - those who are ex-tribe. Whereas the primary motivation of other groups is the creation of unity and a sense of home.

Whether the group is large enough to spread across the globe, or so small that its members number in the single digits, there are similarities in how each tribe identifies its members and separates itself from the rest of the world.

Common languages are used and differ from the spoken words of other bands of people. Ideas and philosophies about concepts such as acceptable behavior, group cohesion, and the tribe's purpose work as well for a small business as they do for the European Union.

The average size of a US high school is just under 800 students. Within those 800 students it is easy to find a large number of different tribes. If you were to sit down in the cafeteria during any lunch period you could observe the break down of jocks, gamers, skaters, stoners, choir kids, goths, and myriad other small and distinct groups.

Each of these little tribes has its own leaders, its own rituals, its own goals, and its own aesthetic.

The school itself is a tribe. The athletic teams identify themselves as the "us" while the athletes who play the same sport but attend a different school are the "them." Colors, fight songs, mascots, and cheers all serve as ways to separate the different groups.

Many of those who don't identify with the school in general, will have their tribal alliances supersede the geographic boundaries of that particular group. Skaters from one neighborhood may have more friends who attend a different school than their own.

Even without hearing a word of conversation, it is easy for an outsider to walk through the halls and identify the distinct groups - because each little tribe has its uniform.

Everyone has a uniform.

The chess club members don't dress the same as the cheerleaders, who have a different appearance than the drama club, who all contrast sharply from the goths. There may be some perceivable similarities, but each band of allies will intentionally and deliberately dress in a way that separates them from any group whom they consider to be ex-tribe.

Cultures and counter cultures, the mainstream and the rebellious, all subconsciously create a uniform which is used to signal to both their in-group and the rest of the world, who they are and the brotherhood to which they belong.

When worn in the correct context, a group's uniform communicates status, respect, and confidence.

When worn in the incorrect context, a group's uniform communicates being an outsider, lack of understanding, and disrespect for the established norms of the tribe - think of a cowboy hat and boots on Wall Street vs a pinstripe suit at a rodeo.

And, while the primary purpose of a tribe's aesthetic is to visually separate "us" from "them," the nuances and variations within their clothing help establish and communicate hierarchy and value within the group.

Take the military as an example. Each soldier in the army wears the same uniform. However, there are patches, medals, and other variations on that uniform that indicate rank, accomplishments, and other measures of service and dedication.

To an outsider, all the men look largely the same and it can be difficult to distinguish between those of different rank. However, to a man steeped within the culture and the tribe of the military, recognizing and valuing these subtle differences in the uniform is not only simple, it's necessary.

Organizations which are less formal or hierarchal may seem as if they don't have visual or aesthetic expressions of standing and rank within the group. But once again, this is only the case for an outside observer who isn't fully immersed in the tribe and its culture.

Signals of status within a community - especially a loosely organized one like a high-school clique or different departments in a large office - can be distinguished when watching those who appear to lead the group.

These are the individuals who will be the early adopters of a trend. They are willing to take a social risk and wear something that slightly varies from the current uniform of the group. Their willingness to do so, coupled with their already-high status within the tribe is a demonstration of confidence and courage and makes the other lower-ranked members want to emulate the clothing and behavior.

Eventually more and more members begin to adopt the new variations on the uniform, until eventually even the newest, lowest person on the totem pole has caught on and is dressing similarly.

At this point, it becomes necessary for the leaders to seek out a new in-tribe status symbol, and the cycle starts all over again.

Now, you may be asking yourself if this is a fixed cycle. Does this mean you have to be trendy in order to be powerful? Are there organizations and tribes that aren't impacted by changes in clothing and appearance? How long do these cycles last?

The answer to all of these is - it depends. Some tribes will be more aesthetically driven than others. Some will see quicker cycles and some will only see minimal, begrudging aesthetic changes.

What's important for you is to recognize the prevalence and pacing of these cycles, along with how changeable the patterns are, within your own given tribes and then to create an appropriate strategy.

If every member of the military started wearing the four stars of a general, it would become necessary to create new representations of rank within the group. However, the military has a strict hierarchy with an established set of guidelines necessary for increasing rank and wearing of new tokens.

This is not the case for tribes with soft standings. If the lead singer of a gutter-punk band shows up to a concert with a bright green mohawk, there's nothing to prevent anyone else in the band or even the audience from adopting the same hair style.

The fluidity of these markers of status not only makes them more difficult to distinguish to an outsider, it also makes them more taboo to discuss among the insiders.

This unwillingness to openly discuss status and its symbols occurs because the lower members of the group want to appear as if their adoption of the trend or token is natural - or even that they naturally and effortlessly implement or embrace the change - not that they're consciously aware of their status (or lack thereof) within the group and want to improve their standing amongst their peers.

But, when it comes to clothing and its impact within a tribe, status is everything.

On October 15, 1985 Nike released the first Air Jordan sneaker. Three days later, then NBA Commissioner David Stern banned them from professional games because their black-and-red colorway was different from the shoes Michael Jordan's teammates were wearing.

Rather than conceding and falling into line, Jordan continued to wear his signature shoes to each of his games.

A battle ensued in which Commissioner Stern fined Jordan $5,000 each time he violated the NBA's rules and wore the shoes. And, without hesitation, Jordan broke that rule each game - eventually leading to a total fine of $410,000

Rather than Jordan paying the fine out of his own pocket, Nike covered each of the penalties and used the controversy to help promote and sell the shoes - leading to sales numbers that were previously unattainable.

Eventually Stern relented and the Air Jordan went on to become the most popular shoe in NBA history. In 2015, the 30th version of the shoe was released and each iteration has become a relevant component of tribal signaling for sneakerheads and basketball fans alike.

But Jordan's impact on fashion in the NBA wasn't just limited to shoes.

Before becoming a professional player, he played college basketball for the University of North Carolina from 1981 to 1984. During this time, the standard length of shorts was well above the knee, and Jordan wore the same uniform as the other men on his team.

Upon turning pro, he wanted to keep his college days close so he wore his UNC shorts beneath his Bulls attire. However, this presented a problem - his UNC shorts wouldn't fit beneath his uniform, so he had to wear baggy, knee-length shorts instead.

That little, practical decision ended up changing the appearance of the entire league. Because so many players - both professional and not - wanted to "be like Mike" (a line from a popular ad in his prime) the baggy short became a staple of the league and eventually even Western society in general.

Contrast Jordan and his aesthetic impact with that of one of his teammates - Dennis Rodman - a man certainly well known at the same time, who dressed in a way that was even more polarizing than Jordan's.

Rodman's signature look was brightly colored hair, a smattering of tattoos, multiple piercings, and the go-to-hell attitude that comes with them. And, although he did have his own contingent of loyal fans, signature shoes, and a successful NBA career, his style never took root - it was never emulated or embraced by other players or fans.

His appearance was always uniquely his. While he was well known and easily recognized, kids didn't line up to buy his shoes, nor did he become a huge household name.

So why was Michael Jordan able to have such an unequaled impact on not only the appearance of the NBA, but fashion in general, while Dennis Rodman had no perceivable impact?

The first reason is very simple - Jordan had higher status.

And status within a tribe changes everything.

Remember the story "The Emperor's New clothes" by Hans Christian Andersen?

It's about two weavers who make a suit for the emperor made from a cloth which is invisible to people who are incompetent, stupid, or unfit for their relative positions.

For fear of being perceived as any of the above, the whole court - and even the emperor himself - disregard what they see with their eyes and exclaim the beauty of the cloth to all around them.

Once the suit is finished, the vain emperor doesn't merely want to show it to his inner court, but parades it to the entire city.

Each attendee of the parade goes along with the farce for fear of being called foolish or incompetent. Only when a small girl openly acknowledges that the ruler isn't wearing anything at all does the crowd turn on the emperor and ridicule him for waltzing around naked.

The interesting thing about this story is that there is no true hero. The little girl who comments on the nudity of the emperor doesn't do so in an act of open rebellion to his status or its displays - she does so because she's too young to understand the nuances of what's happening around her.

The people who are emboldened to call the suit what it is - nothing - are only willing to do so once another person has broken rank and granted them permission to do the same.

At the end of the tale, the emperor continues believing in the value of the suit. He's convinced himself, and those around him, that it's working as intended and only children and fools cannot see the beautiful cloth - he clings to the demonstration of his status even when it's obvious that it is a lie.

As demonstrated by both Jordan and the emperor, the higher your status, the more you can dress in a way that counters the uniform of your tribe.

The lower your status, the more dressing against the norm conveys social retardation, rather than rebellion worth emulating.

This lack of social fluency, knowing where you fall within the tribe or within civilization in general, often leads to dressing in a way that becomes more of a liability than an asset.

No one is going to start following a trend started by a loan officer at your local bank. But people will wait in line for hours and pay thousands of dollars to dress like Kanye West. The difference between the two lies in their relative status.

A great demonstration of this principle can be seen in a mistake many men make when abandoning their cargo shorts and T-shirts. They often start dressing up like a gentleman from a time when men in general had high social status - think of the stereotypical middle-class, white-collar worker in the United States during the 1950's and 60's.

This uniform made sense in a time where all high-status men dressed in a way that was very uniform. The President wore similar clothes to business tycoons, who dressed almost identically to film stars.

But because style evolves and because that 50's example of masculinity is no longer something our modern culture looks up to, the current attempts at dressing better by adopting an old-school style end up looking more like wishful thinking, anachronism, or cosplay.

As our global civilization becomes increasingly more diverse in status displays there is no set standard of what a high-value man looks like.

Athletes, celebrities, politicians, entrepreneurs, business executives, and online influencers - the high-status men of the 21st century have no common aesthetic ground between them. There is no singular look, style, or appearance that tells the same story wearing a crisp suit did 60 years ago.

Dressing differently is one way for high-status individuals to check their social currency. If they adopt a different style and people follow suit, it's a good indicator that they are still elevated in the social pecking order. If people don't, then it lets them know their position is slipping.

Dressing differently is also an excellent way for up-and-comers to solidify their new high status. What these men can back up with skill, resources, or charm often goes ignored unless it's signaled by dressing and acting differently from everyone else.

On November 12, 2016 Conor McGregor became the first UFC fighter in history to simultaneously hold two championships. The rise from his first pro fight to making history was meteoric and it was accompanied - and even propelled - by his unique relationship with clothing.

The UFC, like nearly every other tribe, has a natural expectation of the way its participants dress. This isn't a hard rule codified by the organization itself, but a natural expression that's evolved as different men have been involved in the sport.

Prior to McGregor coming in and shaking things up, most of the fighters dressed very similarly - at press conferences, interviews, or just on the street. Their style was unassuming, heavily branded with sponsors logos, and they typically wore the same clothes outside of the gym as in.

While there were a few outliers who dressed distinctly - and even built personal brands around unique items like cowboy hats and others, the culture of the sport didn't start to change until McGregor changed it.

Shortly after winning his first pro fight, McGregor started attending press conferences and media events in bespoke suits and couture casual wear. When his competitors were wearing "Tap Out" t-shirts, McGregor was wearing Gucci bit loafers.

This could have been simply another way for an average fighter to make himself a more memorable character but McGregor had both the confidence and the fighting ability to change the landscape of the organization. His out-of-the-cage style quickly became part of his personal brand and helped him signal his rise in status to his opponents.

McGregor has a big ego, a big mouth, and the skills to back both up, so it only makes sense that he would use loud, ex-tribe clothing as a way to communicate to the rest of the fighters in his sport that he believes he is better than they.

Now that his clothing and lavish lifestyle have become an expectation and have even been copied and adopted by other fighters, McGregor has found himself adapting his clothing again.

And even in this, he's demonstrating a better understanding of how clothing can be used to signal status within his tribe.

You see, by embracing red roll necks and white mink coats like those worn by Joe Frazier, or the Coogi sweaters worn by Muhammad Ali, McGregor is copying the unique style of the sport's legends and telling the world that he belongs in their company - that he's earned the right to dress like them because he can fight as well as they did.

When the rest of the sport started rising to McGregor's sartorial level, he stepped up his game and started to look like the gods of the ring.

When we compare the examples of Conor McGregor and Dennis Rodman, it's easy to see some similarities and differences. Both used the same approach of dressing in an iconoclastic way as part of building a personal brand; both signaled a level of antipathy for the clothing standards of the tribe; and both leveraged their unique appearance to rise higher in the ranks of their sport than they may have otherwise.

However, unlike Rodman, McGregor's skill set was strong enough to get him recognized as the top participant of his sport. This high status - in both ability and clothing - is why more men in the UFC started to adopt McGregor's style and branding than NBA players did with Rodman.

For McGregor, the clothing was part of the overall champion. For Rodman, it was the primary thing that made a player much more interesting than those in the league with the same skill level.

By pairing up a drastic style with high levels of mastery, you can dictate the trends of the tribe. Otherwise you'll simply be a unique character on the fringes.

Both McGregor and Rodman were rebels - not leaders like Jordan. But McGregor's influence is broader simply because he has the mastery and ability to complement his outlandish style.

For iconoclasts like McGregor and Rodman, their clothing is a way to separate themselves from the tribe, disincentivize a desire to copy their style, and make sure they aren't easily forgotten or glossed over. They want to be different and they dress uniquely in order to facilitate that.

If rebels like McGregor and Rodman want to dress drastically differently, then leaders like Jordan should only seek to subtly separate themselves. This gives plausible deniability to would-be followers who can claim to adopt the style for purely practical or aesthetic reasons - not because they're lower in the social hierarchy and are trying to increase their perceived value by dressing more like the new leader.

To make this even more complicated, status and style are always evolving - in both soft and established hierarchies. In fact, this constant evolution is why trends come and go.

In a soft hierarchy, say one that's determined by musical interest or income in the West, men use their clothing as a way to signal and reinforce where they fall within that hierarchy, even if its unintentional.

Those who are higher up the ladder dress in a way that sets them apart from those beneath them. It may be something subtle like changing from a narrow lapel on a suit to one that's wider.

For a period there will be some mild rejection of the wider lapel by the rest of the tribe who is used to wearing one which is narrower. They'll see it as off-trend, outdated, or simply obtuse.

But, if enough high-status men jump over to a wider lapel, then the power of social proof kicks in. Those who are slightly lower on the totem pole than the trend setters will recognize lapel width as one of the things that separates them from the top echelon within the culture and will start to adopt the style.

And once the second and third-tier members embrace the wider lapel, that same social proof continues to increase in power and momentum. Very quickly a wider lapel will go from being a risky aesthetic decision to being a trend. Then it will become more and more commonplace and evolve from being a trend to being an expectation.

Once the lowest status members embrace the wide lapel and it is no longer an effective means of communicating where a man falls within the hierarchy, the cycle starts over again with some new change the high-status, risk-comfortable men embrace.

Feeling exhausted yet? Does this mean you have to chase trends for the rest of your life? Well, yes and no. Thankfully the life cycle of these changes can be long - often spanning over decades. So don't think that you have to completely replace your wardrobe each and every year in order to reap the benefits of dressing intentionally.

Clothing and its navigation are not just used as intra-tribal signals. They are also an effective tool in marking distinctions inter-tribally.

Cultures that are uninterested in cohesively working with other groups typically dress in ways that immediately set them apart from the world around them. This is especially true in religious organizations - Orthodox Jews, Buddhist monks, the Amish, fundamentalist Mormons, devout Muslims, or any other devoted members of a unique faith dress in a way that intentionally separates them from the rest of the world.

But this isn't just limited to religious organizations. The same pattern is found in motorcycle clubs, social justice warriors, gutter punks, and prison gangs. The more a tribe rejects greater society as a whole, the more they will signal that rejection through their aesthetic decisions and priorities.

I experienced this first hand as a member of the punk scene of the late 90's and early 2000's. Looking back, the cognitive dissonance was comical. Every time I'd have an argument with my parents about the way I was dressing, I would inevitably tell them I didn't care what I looked like. But backpacks with the perfect balance of safety pins and band patches, T-shirts that only sported logos from my favorite bands and BMX companies, black hair that was spiked just right way, and pants that had the perfect sag never happened by accident.

These little details took immense thought and effort to execute in a way that was acceptable to my tribe and helped them embrace me as one of their own, not an outsider who was posing or pretending.

Had I ever had the audacity to show up in an outfit looking like an ivy-league kid or some other stereotype of "the man" I would have been immediately and effectively ostracized from my entire circle of high-school friends.

Appearance currently matters more to subcultures and their members than it does to those who generally see themselves as happy and fitting into society in general. But that hasn't always been the case.

Take, for example, sumptuary laws and how they were used to enforce social hierarchies by restricting luxury, consumption, and displays of wealth. Black's Law Dictionary defines them as "Laws made for the purpose of restraining luxury or extravagance, particularly against inordinate expenditures in the matter of apparel, food, furniture, etc."

The laws were often created to prevent commoners from attempting to appear like the aristocracy and to facilitate ostracization by stigmatizing unfavorable groups.

Essentially, when these laws were in effect during the late middle ages, their primary purpose was to help nobility separate themselves from the bourgeoisie, and for the bourgeoisie to distinguish themselves from every one beneath them.

These cultures understood that the furniture people owned, the food they ate, and the clothes they wore were all direct ways of communicating where and how well a man fit within or stood out from various groups.

While we are thankfully free from such heavy-handed laws today, it does not mean the principles upon which those laws were founded carry any less weight now than centuries ago.

And no, we do not live in a strictly delineated caste system (at least in the modern West) but we do still naturally separate ourselves into various groups and then use various markers as way to signal our relationships with others around us.

Some may lament this and claim that the ability to dress distinctly is the cause, and the class, group, or tribal separation is the effect. Both historical and fictional examples of authoritarian regimes are filled with instances of a version of a State uniform being implemented in order to ensure no one separates himself, or his group, from anyone else.

But the clothing isn't the cause, it's merely one of the many ways group distinction and, even further, individuality are expressed to those around us.

10 TASTE

Think about the last time you heard someone do an accurate impersonation of another person - celebrity or otherwise. What is it that made the portrayal so spot on?

They probably adopted the same vocal tone, body language, cadence, emphases, and sentence structure of the person they were were imitating.

For some people, each of those things may be uniquely their own. But for most, each individual element about the way we speak is something we see in others around us.

Think about the last time you went to a great restaurant. I'm not talking about the lighting, service, or people you were with - although those all contribute to a wonderful dining experience - I'm simply talking about fantastic food.

If you were to go back watch the food being prepared, do you think there would be any ingredients that have never been used in food before?

Does a unique dish have to be unique because the chef uses soil, wool, or some other non-food ingredient in it?

Obviously not. What does make it unique is either a new combination of existing ingredients, or an existing combination of ingredients simply using them in different proportions.

It's what separates good cooks from great chefs. A good cook will use all of the simple ingredients in safe and proper proportions. Whereas a great chef will either pull in an ingredient that hasn't been tried with a particular dish, or play around with proportions until he finds something that makes the perfect meal.

I'm sure you can see where I'm going with this.

Taste isn't so much about wearing things no one else has worn before as it is about combining components of your various tribes, hobbies, beliefs, and identities into your unique presentation.

To go back to the idea of clothing being communication - Taste isn't inventing a new language, accent, or specific words - it's creating idioms, catch phrases, and speech patterns.

One of the easiest ways to observe Taste is as a parent - both in speech and in dress.

When my oldest daughter was two, she was in the habit of saying, "Let's do this!" whenever we told her we were going somewhere or doing something different.

It was fun to hear because it reflected her enthusiasm for life and also because she sounded a lot more grown up than she was.

She wouldn't simply say the words. She spoke them with the same speed and the same emphasis every time she uttered the phrase.

My wife and I still laugh when we think about it.

Oddly enough, neither one of us knew where she'd heard the phrase. It was obviously a mimicry of something she'd picked up somewhere but we couldn't figure out where.

It wasn't used by any of the characters on the shows she watched - certainly not frequently enough to plant itself in her brain like that. Nor was it something we associated with any of our friends or family. No one we knew was using this phrase consistently enough for my daughter to adopt it from them.

We remained curious and confused about this until one day when I was out on a photoshoot.

The photographer I was working with had just seen a new spot, pointed it out, and suggested we get over there quickly while the lighting was good. I responded by saying, "Let's do this!" in the exact same way my two year old would.

I realized right then that I was the one she had heard the phrase from. However, it was one I used so absent-mindedly that I never even consciously heard it as I was speaking it. On top of that, it was used often enough that even my wife had stopped hearing me say it and it had become something commonplace.

But, to the two-year-old sponge my child was, it was the obvious and appropriate response for a change in action.

The words I used weren't newly created. They weren't unique in their definition nor was their application something that was more common in my own given tribes than other parts of the English-speaking world.

But, the frequency, tone, cadence, and enthusiasm with which I said them had made them a part of my own particular vernacular - which was picked up by my daughter and became her go-to response as well.

Our Taste in our style and appearance is expressed the same way.

All too often, it's not a deliberate selection of clothing but just the inertia of something we've found that works for us.

It may contain particular elements of our Archetype or Tribe but the frequency and comfort with which we dress can often turn what we wear into a personal uniform.

None of which is bad - but it's also not necessarily good. The best habits and behaviors don't happen by accident. At some point they become automatic, but they have to start with some deliberate thought and action on our part.

The same applies to our appearance. The best style doesn't happen by accident. It eventually becomes automatic and natural, but it has to start with some deliberate thought and action on our part.

Taste can be a false goal in dressing more intentionally. In fact, many men who dress a certain way will use the justification that they like it or it makes them happy and believe that that's the only or the most important aspect of the equation.

Which is not to say that personal preference and affinity for clothing don't have any place in dressing well - they certainly do. But it must be understood that there are tradeoffs which come with prioritizing Taste or personal preference above everything else.

This is fairly easy to see when we look at the physical and functional aspect of our clothing.

For example, if you decided you just loved surfing in a three-piece suit, that would obviously be your decision to make. However, there are obvious trade-offs that would come with that. Your physical ability to surf would likely be impacted, as would your overall comfort in the water.

The goal of the activity - surfing - would be negatively affected by the tactical decision to wear a three-piece suit, making it very easy to see why this isn't common beach attire.

The same can be applied to fur coats in the Sahara or loin cloths in Antarctica. Again, your personal Taste may lean that way, but the physical implications typically override the benefits of dressing entirely according to your Taste.

This is something that is so obvious and automatic that we don't take the time to consciously think about it, nor do we resent its reality.

However, when that same principle is taken outside of the realm of the physical and into the social, the water becomes a bit muddier.

If you were to tell a man who loves wearing bow ties that his decision to do so hurts his chances for success at work, he'd resent you for it. He'd argue that it shouldn't matter and his work should only be impacted by his performance. Or he'd say that the world is too judgmental and he doesn't want to impress those people anyway. Or he might just stop wearing bow ties and stew about wishing he worked in a different environment in which his Taste was more embraced.

Whatever the story we tell ourselves in our head, we often resent or outright reject the potential risks that come from dressing only in accordance with our personal Taste.

We'll talk more in the next chapter about how location and environment both can and should affect our aesthetic choices, but for now let's focus on why the social implications of Taste can be so frustrating for so many men.

At the root of it, the problem exists because we see our identity expressed through out appearance. Not just our own place within the world, but who we are compared to those around us.

If that weren't the case, we either wouldn't factor in our personal Taste at all, or we'd treat the social tradeoffs as matter-of-factly as we do the physical.

If you resent having to alter your personal decisions because of social reasons but not physical ones, then - on some fundamental level - you are concerned with the story you're telling the rest of the world.

And that's a good thing.

Like we've addressed before, people are tribal. We thrive in groups and only the outliers of the world do better off as lone wolves.

If you're like many of the other men I've coached and worked with, you might be feeling a bit resentful of how strong a role Tribe plays in dressing well.

You may be telling yourself that none of that should matter and you should be able to dress however you want.

Or that the most important thing about a particular article of clothing in your closet is that you like it - not that anyone else does.

If you are feeling this way, I completely understand. I've been there myself and I've also helped other men with it as well.

For the most part, we experience a resentment of this for two reasons. The first is that we create a false dichotomy between Taste and Tribe - we tell ourselves that it's either all one or completely the other.

But Taste and Tribe can and do simultaneously co-exist. In fact, it's not all that often that they are mutually exclusive.

The second reason is that we believe that somehow prioritizing Taste over Tribe is morally superior.

It stems from the modern interpretations of honor and integrity along with other terms like authenticity.

To best illustrate this, I'll refer to Donovan again as he illustrates the seeming differences between individuality and cooperation or, in our aesthetic terms, Taste and Tribe:

> Men who want to avoid being rejected by the gang will work hard and compete with each other to gain the respect of the male gang. Men who are stronger, more courageous and more competent by nature will compete

with each other for higher status within that group. As long as there is something to be gained by achieving a higher position within the gang—whether it is greater control, greater access to resources or just peer esteem and the comfort of being higher in the hierarchy than the guys at the bottom—men will compete against each other for a higher position. However, because humans are cooperative hunters, the party-gang principle scales down to the individual level. Just as groups of men will compete against each other but unite if they believe more can be gained through cooperation, individual men will compete within a gang when there is no major external threat but then put aside their differences for the good of the group. Men aren't wired to fight or cooperate; they are wired to fight and cooperate.

Understanding this ability to perceive and prioritize different levels of conflict is essential to understanding The Way of Men and the four tactical virtues. Men will constantly shift gears from in-group competition to competition between groups, or competition against an external threat.

It is good to be stronger than other men within your gang, but it is also important for your gang to be stronger than another gang. Men will challenge their comrades and test each other's courage, but in many ways this intragroup challenging prepares men to face intergroup competition. Just as it is important for men to show their peers they won't be pushed around, the survival of a group can depend on whether or not they are willing push back against other groups to protect their own interests. Men love to show off new skills and find ways to best their pals, but mastery of many of the same skills will be crucial in battles with nature and other men.

I know that's a lot to chew on and Donovan is speaking much more on how things like strength and mastery contribute to your position within your Tribe.

However, what must always be understood is that your appearance - whether that's your clothing, body language, posture, body markings, or any other visual signal, is one of the primary ways in which you help others in the gang know where you fall within the hierarchy.

Just as men are wired to both compete against and cooperate with other men in their tribe depending on the circumstances, your appearance can be directed to either compete against (Taste) or cooperate with (Tribe) the other men in the gang.

Knowing when and how to navigate these nuances requires a certain level of mastery - the signaling of which can bolster both your own individual position within your tribe, and your overall tribe's position in the rest of the world.

Taste, when done properly can be almost impossible to distinguish from someone who is ex-tribe - although it doesn't necessarily have to be.

Going back to a previous comparison, another big difference between a good cook and a great chef is the chef also fails more often.

It comes with the territory of moving outside of the normally accepted realm of behavior. Not every dish is going to be an award-winning recipe. In fact, most will be bad - at least at first. But as he becomes more and more experienced and adept at creating new ratios or completely new combinations, his failures will decrease and his successes will become more frequent and stronger.

The chef has to be willing to put in the time and energy to overcome those failures and turn them into successes.

You have to do the same thing with your appearance, but there's another component which exists with clothing that we don't find in food.

If the chef ruins a dish, no one else has to taste it. He can practice at home, in private in order to attain the level of mastery he's striving for.

He's also able to depend almost entirely on his own taste buds for accurate feedback. So not everyone will need to be exposed to his poor recipes in order for him to understand they're not great and begin to improve them.

But this is not true with style. In order to test the waters and truly know if you can pull off a particular look or style, you need to wear it. In public. With people reacting to it. You need to get feedback - both direct and indirect - from those around you, to know if you've properly told your story and balanced out the Tribe and Taste components necessary for good style.

With appearance, you don't have the luxury of practicing, failing, and improving in a bubble. And this is ultimately why so many men never improve. The social risk is too great and their perception of the potential payoffs is too low to justify the backlash that can come while in the learning curve.

But again, this fear is based on a false assumption. Many of these men assume that their Taste will ultimately require them to start wearing outlandish pieces - things that will set them apart and make them visually interesting. While this may be one component of introducing a personal flavor into your appearance, it's not the only one.

The other approach to Taste is to realize it's not always about adding new elements, but can often be about removing things we commonly see. Taste is more about digesting the elements of Tribe into something more unique than it is about adding something in that's completely new and unheard of.

A simple T-shirt and jeans can be both stylish and unique when they fit right, are made from quality materials, and are used to properly express the variations between Tribe and Taste for the man wearing them.

Standing out for its own sake or at the complete expense of other factors of a masculine appearance is rarely a good thing. It doesn't matter what your personal taste is, how much social courage you have, or how little you care for the expectations of your various tribes. If you dress in a plastic garbage bag every day, it will have a negative impact on your success as a man. Even Conor McGregor, Michael Jordan, and the fictional emperor couldn't pull that look off.

This is why Taste comes after Tribe in the hierarchy of dressing well. Taste can expand upon, twist, or combine tribal elements, but it can never fully supersede the importance of how others perceive what we wear.

11 LOCATION

Does whispering in a library mean you have no integrity? Are you not being true to yourself if you use different language in a church than you do at a sporting event?

Are you an inconsistent person when you use larger words around adults than you do with children?

Of course not! We know that different language is appropriate in different environments - even if we're surrounded by the same people. And there's nothing wrong with or inconsistent about adapting your language to the expectations of your location.

Here's another question - what do Eskimos and Aborigines have in common?

They both dress in a way that is entirely appropriate for their environment.

In fact, living in these extreme parts of the world often makes location and environment the most important aspects of how they dress.

For example, in order to survive in the extreme climate of the far north, the Eskimo natives of Alaska developed clothing called Yup'ik and it is still the the most effective cold-weather clothing created.

It consists mostly of skins and furs from animals like caribou, reindeer, and seal. Even the thread used to stitch the skins together is mostly animal sinew or grass.

The clothing worn by hunters not only needed to be insulated but also waterproof, so they use materials like fish skin and marine mammal intestines to help line parkas, boots, and other articles.

But it wasn't just cold and water that needed to be accounted for. Take, for example, how slippery ice can be. In order to help maximize traction, the soles of Eskimo boots - mukluks - are made from chewed skins of bearded seals.

Even the hunters' headgear is perfectly adapted to help protect his eyes and face from waves, while helping camouflage him from his prey during hunting season.

Waterproof, cold-resistant, ice-adapted clothing was and is necessary in this part of the world.

Contrast this with the traditional clothing of the aboriginal natives of Australia - especially the Eora people who lived in what is now the Sydney area.

They wore no clothing at all because the environment didn't demand it. They were a people who lived mostly off of what they could fish and hunt and did not engage in agriculture.

The climate was inviting enough that clothing was not necessary for protection from the elements or from predators.

That said, the people still wore arm bands and body paint as ways to signal things like status and the tribes they belonged to. Many markings were used for specific religious ceremonies and initiation rites.

Can you imagine what would happen if the two different groups swapped places? How long do you think it would take them to realize their current style of clothing is not only irrelevant, but actually hinders their ability to thrive in their new location within the world.

How long can a naked Eora survive an Alaskan winter? What good are sealskin mukluks while combing the Sydney beaches for crabs or feasting on beached whales?

As much as clothing truly is a social medium - one that has more of an impact on things like status, tribe, self-perception, and aspiration - it still has its roots in the functional relationship between man and nature. It's why we don't typically see overcoats in the jungle, swim trunks in the desert, or sandals on top of Mt. Everest.

Your location and climate needs may not be as extreme as some parts of the world. You may be lucky enough to live in an environment that stays moderately humid and comfortably warm for most of or the entire year.

Or, you may be like me and live in an area that experiences all four seasons in an extreme way. You may see scorching heat in the summer, bone-biting cold in the winter, and a full range of conditions in between.

Either way, do you have what you need in your closet to thrive in these environments? What if you travel?

There's a running joke that everyone in Salt Lake City owns a San Francisco 49ers jacket.

You see, most of us in Utah equate California with Los Angeles, Orange County, and San Diego. When we hear "Cali," we think warm beaches, palm trees, and surfing.

And so, when people from my home town make their way to Northern California, they often pack as if they're headed to Venice Beach - even when traveling there in the dead of winter.

The problem is that California is a large state, and its more northern cities experience a stronger variation in seasons. We in Utah recognize it doesn't snow in the Bay, and then wrongfully assume that the reason it doesn't snow is because it doesn't get cold.

So, when visiting this part of the country, far too many of us pack for summer sunshine and heat waves. It's only upon arrival, that we realize the reality is far different from our expectations and it can often get uncomfortably chilly in the Bay.

And, as a solution, we pick up the first warm layer available to us, a jacket representing a team from a city and state to which we don't belong.

I understand that this is a very niche and targeted example of the importance of understanding location, but the ramifications are applicable everywhere.

I remember my first visit to the Bay. It was January and the temperatures were in the low 50's. We'd just flown out of Utah where we'd had a few recent nights in sub-zero temperatures and the improvement of over 60 degrees was a welcome change.

I spent that first day in the city in a simple pair of jeans and a grey T-shirt. I remember walking into one of the stores of the company I was part of and the immediate reaction of the men running the shop.

"You're crazy! You're dressed like it's summer when it's freezing outside!"

They were layered up in flannel, scarves, and tweed while I was happy to be out of a heavy winter coat and gloves. We were in the same location, but our perception of it and relationship to it were entirely different.

Which brings us to one of the more interesting challenges for modern men. Unlike Eskimos and Aborigines, we're not limited to spending most, if not all, of our lives in one part of the world.

We have access to travel that can take us to locations far beyond our original roots and our wardrobes need to change to reflect those different locations - whether experienced for a short period of time as part of a trip, or as a permanent move.

Location can also have an impact on the overall effect of Tribe.

Most world travelers revel in the idea that food, language, culture, and clothing are different in various parts of the world.

Japan may have a similar climate as France, but the cultural differences between the two are incredibly strong. So strong that even a relatively simple, uniform-like piece of clothing, such as a suit, will look very different in those two locations.

The average man may not be able to label and call out all the distinctions between the way the French wear a suit vs the Japanese, but he would be able to see there is a difference if exposed to one Japanese suit in a sea of French suits or vice versa.

Once clothing moves from something relatively limited like suiting into a realm with more freedom - like casual or historical attire - the differences in location become more dramatic.

Here's another example. I have a friend named David who is originally from North Carolina. He has lived in Utah the past few years and always has people comment on his casual clothes.

The clothing he grew up seeing as normal, innocuous, and simple draws extra attention out here - even though the changes are small and mundane.

Rather than wearing flip-flops in the summer, he chooses boat shoes. His shorts fall just above the knee instead of below it. He prefers to wear Brooks Brothers Oxford cloth button-down shirts instead of T-shirts as his daily uniform.

None of these come anywhere near the location-emphasized cultural differences between a turban or a baseball cap, but they still have an impact on his life and the way he interacts with the people around him.

Like many of the aesthetic variables and choices we've discussed, his decision to maintain his East Coast style in the Intermountain West is neither good nor bad - it just is.

My friend appreciates feeling a little different from those around him. He likes feeling a connection with his roots, and he benefits from the assumptions made about his "dressing better" than what many people in Utah are used to seeing as a default.

However, if he had negative associations with his life and the people back home, if he felt self-conscious about fitting in in his new location, or decided he wanted to embrace the more casual style of the typical Utahan he would quickly and easily adapt his style to those goals.

But, even beyond where you live or what the broader cultural expectations are, location has its own more targeted components as well.

What you wear to the gym should be different than what you wear to work, which should be distinct from what you wear to the movies, and on and on and on.

This level of variation can be taken from one realm of extreme to the other.

Most common is the man who doesn't have any change in his appearance. We've all seen or known people who dress the same for their daily life as they do for special occasions. Sure they may occasionally step it up for something important like a funeral or a wedding, just like they may go a bit more casual than usual for a session with the weights or a day at the pool, but they spend most of their time at a comfortable average with very little fluctuation.

Not as common but still seen are men who need a specific wardrobe for each environment. They have suits that are only worn when meeting with clients, others that only come out when hiring, and others they wear for sales calls.

The average man may not see the difference between these suits or the need for that distinction, but the men who do will see and experience value in those decisions.

Most of us fall somewhere in between these examples.

The average style-conscious man has typically spent some time developing his style based on the already-discussed variables of Body, Taste, Tribe, and overall location.

However, the average style-conscious man has also typically only done this for one location - his primary environment.

It's a trap I've personally fallen into. Over the years I've spent a lot of time developing my suit style. For ten years I wore suits nearly every day. I worked with a company that makes and sells custom suiting, and I run my own business dedicated toward helping men dress better.

Suiting is something I know well and I can do confidently and competently.

But once I'm taken out of that primary environment, once my location and needs shift from work to home, or the gym, or camping, or any of the other occasional, secondary and tertiary locations where I find myself, my style quickly declines.

For many years no one who would have seen me at the gym would have had any idea that I teach men about the importance of appearance. In fact, they probably would have actively resisted that idea because my gym clothes were awful. Those clothes didn't accurately represent my Body, Archetype, Tribe, or Taste. They just did the functional job of properly handling sweat and getting out of my way.

My casual clothes weren't necessarily dropping jaws on Instagram either. And it was because I didn't learn to factor in various locations and environments into my style.

Learning to dress well at work is only one battle - not the entirety of the war. And, while it may be easy to think your appearance shouldn't matter as much at a backyard BBQ as it does in a meeting with a client, it's an erroneous assumption, and one that can easily be tested.

Would you feel as comfortable and confident at a BBQ if you were wearing a suit as you do in your casual clothes? What if you showed up wearing a bathrobe? Unless you're willing to drastically overdress or underdress for a given location, it should be apparent that your appearance matters in any environment and it's worth developing a style that is consistent with your broader goals.

The benefits are geared more toward how you see and carry yourself than how someone else views you. If you're wearing a tank top on the way to the pool, it likely won't be seen as better or worse than a short-sleeved button-up shirt by anyone else who's there.

However, if one of those options helps you recognize yourself as a man of discipline and style, someone who looks and feels great - regardless of the environment, then you should choose that particular style of shirt, rather than settle for the other.

Remember earlier when we talked about the origin and importance of graduation robes? Well the difference between a long black robe, with a bunch of tassels, and a square hat looking like a symbol of respect and accomplishment or like you've gone completely off the deep end is whether you're wearing it to a graduation ceremony or out to pick up groceries.

Environment and location dictate the appropriateness of the clothing.

Both form and function are dictated by the location and environment in which you find yourself. Both need to be considered when getting dressed. Both will make or break your appearance.

12 EFFORT

Who's a more effective communicator, the smooth talker who knows exactly the right word to say at the right time, or the stoic who prefers to say as little as absolutely necessary?

Trick question because neither is objectively better than the other.

How about this? Who's better dressed, the man with a massive wardrobe who has a specific item for every occasion, or the minimalist who only needs to make a few tweaks depending on his needs?

Another trick question because again, neither is objectively better than the other.

So which route should you take - the huge, diverse wardrobe or the minimal one?

Both have their pros and cons, and neither is objectively better or worse than the other. So how do you determine which is subjectively better for you?

And how do you measure the different levels of required effort against each other?

The man with the massive selection may need to take more time getting ready in the morning. His clothing may have taken longer to acquire and cost him more money too. But he also has more opportunities to leverage a specific appearance to a desired outcome. He also may simply find joy in the process of getting dressed each morning and doesn't see it as laborious at all.

In order to truly master your appearance, you need to learn how to apply the ideal amount of effort to get the results you're after.

The ideal goal in any pursuit is effortless mastery. However, the only way to arrive there is through exertion. No one gets to mastery without putting in time, energy, and effort.

A simple wardrobe will require less mastery and therefore, less effort. But it can also be more limiting and not yield as many results. You need to experiment and assess the costs and opportunities that will come into your life with the size of your closet. From there you can determine if you want a bunch of clothes or very few.

Now, if you are like most modern men you are probably a bit loathe to put in any effort beyond the bare minimum toward your appearance. I get it. Like we've addressed earlier in this book, there are both internal motivations and external pressures that make us feel this way.

To better understand this position, we need to first understand the relationship between effort and mastery in any given arena. After all, no one is born a master and even the greats in any field started off as awkward, clumsy beginners.

Here's how the hierarchy of mastery looks.

We begin at a stage in which we have not mastered a given skill set, nor have we put in any effort to do so. The balance between input and output is fine because we're not investing anything and the lack of results is commensurate.

However, if we want to attain any real results, we need to start investing time and energy. This is the second stage and is arguably the worst phase of the entire process. In stage two we have an input of effort with very little positive output. Most average men avoid doing new or challenging things out of an aversion to this stage of the growth process.

Think of the time taken to learn to play the piano. Those first few weeks or months are frustrating, tedious, and discouraging. You're putting in hours of practice yet can barely play a few notes or chords without a mistake. At no point does mastery feel farther away than during this second stage.

Stage two is what separates the dedicated from the passively interested. Sadly quitting at stage two means any effort, time, money, or energy invested into a solution has largely been wasted.

After the grind, results start to come and you enter stage three - proficiency with effort. You're still not a master, but you've made enough progress that you're able to demonstrate a real skill set.

Your input and output are starting to equalize again and both are much higher than they were before you started the growth process.

From there, with a bit more continued effort, that proficiency becomes easier and easier and you enter into stage four - effortless proficiency.

This is the first stage where the balance of input and output finally shifts to your favor. In this effortless proficiency stage, you're able to drop your input level of effort lower than it's been at any point other than the first stage, while still maintaining a higher level of output.

For many, this is the final destination. This is because the benefits of our activity - dressing well, playing the piano, public speaking, playing a sport, etc. - can start to taper off. Rather than following linear growth where more mastery leads to more benefit, the benefits start to mellow even as the mastery improves. Therefore, most men are going to be happy in the proficiency arena.

And there's nothing wrong with that. We don't all need to be Olympic level athletes, billionaire entrepreneurs, and influencers with audiences that number in the millions. For many of us, the effort required to jump up from proficiency to mastery in any arena, let alone all of them, simply shifts the balance between input and output back in a way that doesn't improve our lives.

However, for those who want to push it further and become masters, the two final stages follow the same pattern as those of proficiency - mastery with effort and then effortless mastery. Where once again we see more effort than results and then eventually even greater results with even less effort.

So, as a brief synopsis:

- Stage 1 - No effort and no mastery

- Stage 2 - Invested effort with no mastery

- Stage 3 - Proficiency with effort

- Stage 4 - Effortless proficiency

- Stage 5 - Mastery with effort

- Stage 6 - Effortless mastery

Let's bring this back to dressing better. After all, we know from our discussion of the tactical virtues that Mastery is a core component of masculinity and that men have always used clothing to communicate that mastery in our lives.

However, things start to get a bit meta when it comes to the skill set of dressing intentionally. You can demonstrate two different components of mastery by dressing well (mastery level one) in a way that shows you're accomplished in other arenas (mastery level two).

But, just like attaining any other skill set, proficiency and mastery require some real work. Which is why most men are content to not develop the skill of dressing well. Not only will they have to go through the stage where they're exerting new effort but don't have many positive results to show for it, but their decision to do so with their clothing becomes very public and visible.

You can practice the piano alone in your home without anyone else having to suffer through your missed notes and awkward chords. But you don't get the same luxury with your clothing. No one has to see all of the hours you spend missing free throws, but they will likely notice if your new pants are too tight, too short, or the wrong color. Unless you plan on buying a lot of clothes and only wearing them alone until you know they're right for you, you're going to be exerting effort, learning, and making mistakes in public - a huge deterrent for a lot of men who may have some desire to dress better.

And that's not all. Style is dealt a second blow because mastery isn't as widely celebrated as it is in arenas like sports, finance, fitness, dating, etc. Yes this has changed a bit over the last decade and it's becoming increasingly more acceptable and popular to look up to and respect men who are well-dressed. But it's still always tied in with other desirable masculine traits.

For example, it's easy to comment on James Bond being well-dressed. And that's one of the components that makes him a compelling character and an icon for many men. But if you take away the super spy with charisma, charm, a way with women, and a knack for saving the world, no one really cares how good Bond looks in a suit.

So understanding that stage two in the hierarchy of development is a public affair, not private, and then pairing that up with the fact that mastery in aesthetics isn't entirely valued on its own makes it easy and understandable (although not necessarily respectable) to see why most guys are content to remain average and have that neutral relationship with their style we talked about all the way back in chapter one.

Thankfully, mastery isn't necessary in style and appearance any more than it is in most realms of a man's life. At least, not a true and complete mastery.

In fact, when it comes to dressing well and intentionally, the end goal for most men should be effortless proficiency.

So how do we quantify and define that proficiency? Is it just the fact that you look good every day? Does it have to do with combining colors and patterns, in a pleasing way, or is there more to it than that?

The first thing to understand is that proficiency and mastery can be attained in all five of the previous steps. You can be proficient or a master in using your appearance best in accordance with your body, archetypes, tribes, tastes and locations.

But it goes even further than that. You can become proficient in the dreaded practice of shopping for clothing and finding things that work for you, or in getting ready each day and looking your best, or in knowing exactly what to wear to stand out rather than blend in..

And all of these different arenas of style proficiency are entirely subjective. The goal is to attain the correct amount of proficiency in each arena that will lead to the right balance between effort and output.

Too much effort with zero output is an apparent loss. But maximal effort with maximal output is also a loss (for most men)

We know we can't put in zero effort and gain a maximal output, but we need to find the right balance.

For some men, the right balance between input and output exists in spending a ton of time shopping and building a wardrobe, therefore making it possible to spend very little time thinking about what they're wearing each and every day.

For others, it may be spending the same amount of time shopping and building the wardrobe and then spending even more time getting ready each morning.

For some it may be avoiding shopping as much as possible and then willingly sacrificing some variety in clothing and potential benefits of having a more versatile wardrobe.

There is no right or wrong answer here. It's all dependent on what is best for you, your life, your circumstances.

This whole approach to understanding input and output, efforts and results, would be just fine if we were machines and only functioned based on the pure logic or practical tradeoffs of our labors.

But we're more complicated than that, and there's one final component that makes this whole process either much easier or a whole lot harder - passion.

Now, passion is not the end-all-be-all solution to success in life. Nor am I saying that you need to develop a real sense of passion for dressing well. I'm not.

However, the reason we equate passion with success is simply because it decreases our own perception of the amount of effort we're putting into improving ourselves. Passion and discipline can attain equal results, but passion makes the journey much more enjoyable and feel easier.

Basically, the more love you have for a given endeavor, the less it feels like work - making it much easier to find your way through the effort-filled stages of development into those that are effortless.

Just remember that perceptive ease of effort in input doesn't always equate to the ideal output. I may not be passionate about doing my accounting each month, but having the discipline to get better at it certainly yields better results than if I never improved at all.

At this point you may be thinking about potential ways to improve output without increasing input. And there certainly are ways to do that, as long as you understanding that you're not necessarily decreasing your input, so much as changing what the source of that energy is.

For example, you could have spent thousands of hours trying to break down and understand the concepts I've illustrated in this book. Instead, you chose to exert your energy into reading and retaining the material here, thereby saving yourself time and money in having to figure these things out on your own.

The amount of time may be less than what you would have invested while trying to develop these principles by yourself, but you had to put in the energy necessary to read the book, and pay the money to buy it.

So time decreased, but money and energy increased.

The same goes with any sort of education principle. Going back to the idea of learning to play the piano or competing in a sport, both of those are made significantly faster and easier by choosing to work with an instructor or coach than if you were to try to attain mastery on your own. You pay for lessons, and you still have to put in the time and energy to practice, so your input is still the same, it's just allocated a bit differently - thereby making it easier to handle.

And this is the same approach you should take with your style. You can save yourself some time and energy by joining forums, reading blogs, and watching videos online. You can save yourself even more time and energy by investing a little money into working with a coach. And don't forget to factor in that passion component. Maybe you need the extra help of a coach, forum, or guide to simply get to a level of proficiency because you have no real passion for looking better and simply can see the benefits.

But maybe your passion is already there and you'll be best served by a mentor, a group, or additional information in order to move from proficiency to mastery.

Either way, once again, it's up to you to gauge what the ideal ratio between energy input and mastery output is, not only in levels, but also the way in which your energy is actually applied.

Now, if you're like a lot of other efficiency-minded men, you may be asking why I don't simply recommend you outsource your style to a stylist, your wife, or some other person who is sufficient. After all, I recommend using a coach, so why not make the whole process easier and just outsource it in its entirety?

There's two major reasons I would encourage you to avoid outsourcing your style.

The first is, as we've discussed throughout this entire book, in order for your style to truly work to your advantage, it needs to be an external expression of who and what you are internally.

For the most part, the job of a stylist is to dress you in a way that makes you look current, and currency is a huge thing. It demonstrates cohesion within the tribe and even a level of mastery when it comes to things like social fluency, but it's only one small piece of the puzzle.

A stylist is going to take your style and turn you into a mannequin. There won't be any pulling from who you are on the inside and telling that story through your appearance.

Even those who are the best, will only take it as far as assigning you to a personality profile or archetype, and then making clothing recommendations entirely upon how they interpret that profile.

Unless you're a one-dimensional man who isn't much more than what society has made him, you don't want to look like a mannequin for some stylist and his or her own personal taste - regardless of how well executed that personal taste may be.

I have a client who has worked with some of the best bespoke tailors in the world. They've made him beautiful garments yet he's never truly been happy with them. The reason is simple - it's because they were dressing him up, rather than helping him tell his story.

These men are masters of the cloth. They've written books and influenced millions of men to dress better. But when all was said and done, they were either incapable of or unwilling to see past their own perceptions of what good style was and created garments that made them, not my client happy.

If you're hesitant about feeling fake in your clothing, the absolute last thing you want to do is turn over the power to choose what you wear to someone else.

After all, no self-respecting man let's something as important as his image be determined by some 22-year-old girl who just finished her fashion degree.

Which ties into reason number two - unless you plan on joining a nudist colony, you're going to be wearing clothing, and experiencing the results of said clothing, for the rest of your life.

When it's something that can impact you so largely, and do so on such a day-to-day basis, eventually self-sufficiency - whether in proficiency or mastery - is going to be in your best interest. You feed yourself, bathe yourself, and think for yourself. You should also be dressing yourself.

13 CONCLUSION

In his book *Influence* author Robert Cialdini introduces the Consistency Principle - the idea that we believe in something more firmly once we've committed to it. Part of our human nature is the desire to be seen - both by ourselves and others - as consistent and reliable. Therefore, when we expressly acknowledge a commitment to any given idea, we find ourselves more loyal to it. The expression of commitment increases the internal drive to stick to our guns.

As a result of this consistency principle, one of the reasons improving ourselves can be so difficult is because we see any major change not as progress but as inconsistency.

We hear expressions of this all the time. "He sold out" or "You've changed so much" and "She's not the person I thought I knew" are all subtle ways of expressing discomfort from an apparent lack of consistency.

The problems with this should be fairly obvious. What do you do when your desire to be perceived as consistent outweighs your drive for self improvement? How can you pull yourself out of a rut without being a completely different person than who you used to be?

Most will avoid the apparent disconnect between these two goals by focusing solely on internal improvements. Your boss won't know if you decide to wake up earlier, nor will your wife immediately recognize efforts on your part to be more patient with the kids, so you won't deal with the fallout of inconsistency by choosing to do so.

But at some point, your self improvement is going to become more apparent to the world around you. Your demeanor will improve, your body will look better, your bank account will be bigger, and you will exude more happiness.

It's foolish to want to hide your newfound growth for fear of being incongruent with the man you used to be.

However, what can be difficult about starting with, and just focusing on, internal improvements is that there is no accountability and very few notches by which you can measure your improvement.

So, by knowing you'll eventually have to move over to obvious, visual methods of self-improvement, and by knowing that choosing these methods can help you stay on track more easily, it becomes apparent that it is in your best interest to start off with a visual method of growth - one that can be seen by others and help to weed out those who will resent and criticize your desire to become a better man, rather than support your efforts in doing so.

Now, this may come as a surprise to you, but I'm not going to say the best change you can make is an improvement of your style. It's actually to your physique. The benefits you experience from being in great shape far exceed those that come from improving your wardrobe. But there are two big limitations with focusing only on how your body is functioning.

First, many men struggle with the idea of change in how they are physically built. They come up against this principle of consistency by taking a sour-grapes approach of not wanting to get in better shape.

I myself have experienced it in the past and continue to see it amongst my friends and colleagues.

Those who are skinny but are a little softer in the belly, more often than not, will pursue forms of exercise which they believe will burn fat without adding any muscle - activities like running, biking, and yoga.

When asked about lifting weights a common response is a lack of desire to "bulk up" - evidence of the benefits of having a more muscular physique aside, these men (and myself at a point in my life) reject the idea of putting on visible muscle - not because they deny that it will benefit their lives, but because it's "not who they are." As if, somehow being slender for their teen years and early adulthood means that is the only acceptable way for their bodies to be built.

The same principle but opposite identity often exists for larger men who have a more significant amount of body fat to lose. The primary way they see themselves and others perceive them is as large men.

When these guys start getting in better shape, they're often much more willing to engage in weight training and are even happy to do a little cardio. But they often can't bring themselves to eat less.

Their brains subconsciously tell them that they're big men and need to eat as much as they were before - if not more food - in order to properly sustain the amount of exercise they're now getting. All they need to do is lift more weight and work a little harder and they'll be able to lose the fat without sacrificing any of the muscle size or strength they've developed over the years.

Both types of men have a similar goal in mind and both have to overcome their natural desire to feel and be perceived as consistent in order to truly develop the bodies that will benefit their lives.

The second limitation that exercise and physical transformations have compared to changes through style and grooming is their tendency to happen gradually.

Even extreme diets can take weeks, or up to a couple of months, before any tangible results are achieved. Because the transformation is so slow and subtle, each look in the mirror will look nearly identical to the last. Remember stage two in our progress hierarchy? This is that stage applied to exercise. Each day seems like there is little or no change. It's only after looking back over the days and weeks that the real transformation becomes noticeable.

A new wardrobe often doesn't have that limitation.

When going out and purchasing better clothing, most men don't simply buy the same thing they've always worn but make slight changes to the fit, then the cloth quality, and then the construction, nor are they making these subtle changes week after week.

Instead, major transformations and changes occur. A man can live for decades with clothing that tells one particular story about his goals, ambitions, tribe, taste, discipline, and character - then spend an afternoon shopping and walk out with a wardrobe which signals entirely different characteristics.

Not only are we wired to resist this kind of drastic change in ourselves, but we resent seeing it in others as well. Rather than recognize it for the improvement that it is, we retire back to our desire for consistency - even if we try to hide our desire for comfort by the use of more noble sounding terms like "authenticity" and "individualism."

Dressing well works with the Consistency principle because it's a public statement. We are signaling our tribe, status, ambitions, and more when we dress a particular way. Because we value consistency, this means we either improve our behavior to match our new appearance, or we resent the dissonance between the two and go back to dressing the way we used to.

Cialdini has said, "The commitments most effective in changing a person's self-image and future behavior are those that are active, public, and effortless." Pretty powerful conclusion right there and one that strongly makes the case for dressing better as one of your earliest endeavors towards improving yourself.

By changing your appearance positively, you're actively engaged in something new. It requires energy input and can provide an output relatively quickly.

It's public - very public. What we talked about as an inherent weakness and reason many men avoid dressing better in the previous chapter is actually one of the biggest strengths of focusing on your style. By making a public change, you've planted your flag and are expected to either rise to the new standard you're signaling to yourself and those around you, or slide back into a life of complacency and mediocrity.

And lastly, it's effortless. At least, it can feel effortless. Sure you need to spend some time learning, and shopping, and failing and succeeding, but dressing better is not an activity that will have to consume your mind, your conversations, or your time. It won't prevent you from spending time with friends and family, it won't take mental energy away from work and hobbies. In fact, it will very quickly start to improve your other activities, goals, and endeavors and help make them start to feel a bit more effortless.

Either way, your appearance is either an asset or a liability, so why not make it the best asset it possibly can be?

RESOURCES

Enclothed Cognition: Adam Hajo, Adam D Galinsky. Journal of Experimental Social Psychology, Volume 48, Issue 4

The Halo Effect: Edward Thorndike. A Constant Error in Psychological Ratings

The Way of Men: Jack Donovan. Dissonant Hum. 2012

Dressing the Man: Alan Flusser. HarperCollins Publishers. 2002

On Killing: Lieutenant Colonel Dave Grossman. Back Bay Books. 1995

Influence: Dr. Robert B Cialdini. William Morrow & Company. 1984

ABOUT THE AUTHOR

Tanner Guzy is based out of Salt Lake City, Utah where he lives with his wife and three children. He has spent the better part of a decade writing about and working within the men's style industry and has a passion for diving into the why's and how's of the world. When he's not creating content for YouTube or other social media platforms, he can be found boxing, playing video games, debating with friends, volunteering with his church, or - most importantly - spending time with his family.

If you'd like to keep up with him, he can be found on Instagram, Twitter, and other social media platforms under @tannerguzy

Printed in Great Britain
by Amazon